FREE, ADULT, UNCENSORED

THE LIVING HISTORY
OF THE
FEDERAL THEATRE PROJECT

SET DESIGN BY HOWARD BAY FOR *LIFE AND DEATH OF AN AMERICAN*

FREE, ADULT, UNCENSORED

THE LIVING HISTORY
OF THE
FEDERAL THEATRE PROJECT

Foreword by

JOHN HOUSEMAN

Edited by

JOHN O'CONNOR *and* LORRAINE BROWN

NEW REPUBLIC BOOKS ■ WASHINGTON, D.C.

First published in 1978 in the United States
by New Republic Books
1220 19th St., N.W.
Washington, D.C. 20036

The authors wish to thank the copyright holders for permission to use the following material:

On pp. 28, 40, 49, the excerpts from *Run-Through*. Copyright © 1972 by John Houseman. Reprinted by permission of Simon & Schuster, a division of Gulf & Western Corporation, and by permission of Russell and Volkening as agents for the author.

On p. 43, the excerpt from *Voices Offstage*. Copyright © 1968 by Mark Connelly. Reprinted by permission of Holt, Rinehart and Winston, Publishers.

On pp. 8, 31, 71, 186, 217, the excerpt from Brooks Atkinson's review, the quote from J. Parnell Thomas, the excerpts from Eugene O'Neill's interview, the cartoon by Don Freeman, and the quote from John Martin's review. Copyright © 1936/38/39 by the New York Times Company. Reprinted by permission.

On p. 165, the Howard Bay set design for the Vassar Production of *One-Third of a Nation* is used by courtesy of the Harvard Theatre Collection.

Library of Congress Cataloging in Publication Data
Main entry under title:
Free, adult, uncensored.
   Includes index.
   1. Federal Theatre Project.   I. O'Connor,
John, 1946-   II. Brown, Lorraine, 1929-
PN2266.F66   792'.022   78-9292
ISBN 0-915220-37-7
ISBN 0-915220-38-5 pbk.

Trade distribution by Simon and Schuster
A division of Gulf & Western Corporation
New York, N.Y. 10020
Ordering No. 24584, 24585 (pbk.)
Printed in Japan

To the men and women who were the Federal Theatre Project

ACKNOWLEDGMENTS

T HIS BOOK IS intended both as a tribute to the many people who made the Federal Theatre Project a significant and lasting contribution to the American theatre and as a sampler for the rest of us so that we can begin to learn what the Federal Theatre Project truly was. We came to write this book as an extension of our work at the Research Center for the Federal Theatre Project, which is dedicated to the preservation and active use of the FTP records. The Research Center was established in 1974 when the Library of Congress deposited the FTP records at George Mason University with the understanding that we would organize the collection, which had been virtually inaccessible since the Federal Theatre ended.

The history of the FTP records, like the Project itself, is one of troubles. When the Federal Theatre closed abruptly in June 1939, no provisions were made for the material that had accumulated. The lighting equipment, costumes, and puppets were sold, assigned to other governmental agencies, or given away. The massive records of the Project were sent to the Library of Congress, the National Archives, and some public libraries. Much of the New York City Project's records went to Vassar where for two years they were used for Hallie Flanagan's excellent history of the FTP, *Arena*. A significant portion of the scene and costume designs stayed in private hands. Through District of Columbia WPA funds, the Library of Congress was able to begin sorting and identifying the material, but the funding was cut in 1941 with the task unfinished. During World War II all "archival" material—correspondence and official records—were transferred to the National Archives, where they are still housed. The "product" material—scripts, posters, designs, notebooks, and research material of various sorts—remained at the Library of Congress. In the post-war and cold-war years, the FTP and its records were ignored as much as possible; the Depression and the "red" label insured that the whole thing was best forgotten. In 1964 the collection was shipped from the Library of Congress, which was badly pressed for space, to an airplane hanger leased as a warehouse. For the next decade it remained there untouched.

In the spring of 1973 we began our search for the Federal Theatre papers. Our initial inquiries were frustrating and futile. The collection seemed to have dropped out of sight. We were temporarily discouraged by a 1949 report that recommended that most of the material be destroyed, but it was unclear whether the recommendations had been followed. Then Lorraine met John Cole, a research librarian at the Library of Congress, who was interested in the WPA Arts Projects and had been working on a rough inventory of the material. He took us to the hangar/warehouse where we found six thousand play and radio scripts, dozens of cabinets of photographs, production notebooks, and play reader reports, crates of posters and set and costume designs, and even seven file cabinets full of newspaper clippings that were the base of the living newspaper morgue. We were ecstatic—the material was in excellent condition and there was more than we had ever imagined (over 800 cubic feet).

The Librarian of Congress, L. Quincy Mumford, deposited the collection at George Mason University, where we would unpack, sort and identify it, and eventually make a register. Then president of George Mason, Vergil Dykstra, agreed to provide basic funds and staff for a Research Center. In 1976 a substantial two-year grant from the National Endowment for the Humanities permitted us to organize the collection and make it available to researchers sooner than we hoped. The grant also supported an extensive oral history program (which is still going on) that allowed us to record the recollections and opinions of former Federal Theatre personnel throughout the country.

In the process of this work we have, of course, been helped by many people who have been generous, patient, and encouraging in their support of our work. This book can only be a partial show of our thanks. We would particularly like to thank Vergil Dykstra, Robert Krug, and Ralph Baxter of George Mason University for their support of the Research Center and our work; Alan Fern, John Cole, and William Sittig of the Library of Congress for their continual cooperation and assistance; Michael Sundell, the Director of the Research Center, for his ideas, drive, and foresight; and Elizabeth Walsh, our curator, for her steadfastness and warmth. A number of people helped us on this book and we are indebted to them: Mae Mallory Krulak who helped formulate the idea of this book, Louanne Wheeler who helped select the plays and oral histories, Karen Wickre who compiled the index, and Jane Keys who typed each draft. We would also like to thank Howard Bay and the National Archives, through Caryl Marsh, for lending us set and costume designs that are not part of the Research Center collection. Special thanks goes to our editor Joan Tapper who took our rough ideas and prose and transformed them into something we are proud of, and to our designer Susan Marsh who has made this book a beautiful one. Finally, we would like to thank our families for their forbearance and encouragement.

FOREWORD

I AM DELIGHTED each time a new book is written and published about the Federal Theatre of the WPA. For close to forty years the only available accounts of that amazing enterprise were Hallie Flanagan's *Arena* and the scattered personal memories of those who had known the excitement of working there. With the recent exhumation of the Federal Theatre archives (now housed at George Mason University in Fairfax, Virginia) a new crop of authoritative studies is promised—of which this is one of the first. The Federal Arts Project and the Federal Theatre, in particular, are of enormous historical and cultural importance and it is time we learned more about them.

Belatedly, in this country, subsidy of the arts is becoming recognized as a national necessity: it has expanded from federal endowment to the activities of state arts councils, and, finally, to the growing participation of industry. There is a lingering tendency to trace this movement back to the Federal Arts projects of the Roosevelt administration. This is an error and an injustice to one of the most remarkable and unique social experiments in our national history—the New Deal's Works Progress Administration.

The Federal Arts projects were a very small part of a vast emergency relief program created to deal with the millions of American citizens who, during the mid-thirties of this century, depended for their survival on public charity. To Harry Hopkins, head of the WPA, goes credit for the notion that those people might be less wretched and discontented if their relief checks were issued in the form of a salary for work accomplished within their own skills and occupations. In September of 1935 (amid cries of socialism, communism, and worse), five billion dollars of federal funds were allocated to the Works Progress Administration for this purpose. Of this a minute portion—less than 1 percent—was devoted to the arts, including the theatre. "It was a relief measure pure and simple conceived in a time of misery and despair. Its only artistic policy was the assumption that thousands of indigent theatre people were eager to work and that millions of Americans would enjoy the results of this work if it could be offered at a price they could afford to pay."

The miracle of the Federal Theatre lies precisely in this—that from the drab and painful relief project there sprang the liveliest, most innovative and most original theatre of its era. This was no accident. "To those who were fortunate enough to be part of the Federal Theatre it was a unique and thrilling experience. Added to the satisfaction of accomplishing an urgent and essential social task in a time of national crisis, it enjoyed the special exhilaration that is generated on those rare and blessed occasions when the theatre is suddenly swept into the mainstream of its time."

In our excitement and satisfaction over our achievements there were those who came to believe—as I professed to believe—that the Federal Theatre had a future. The most lucid and vocal of these optimists was our leader Hallie Flanagan, the remarkable woman to whose visionary obstinancy the Project owed so much of its energy. She thought and spoke of the Federal Theatre as a lasting and permanent thing: "While our immediate aim is to put to work thousands of theatre people, our more far-reaching purpose is to organize and support theatrical enterprises so excellent in quality and low in cost and so vital to the communities involved that they will be able to continue after federal support is withdrawn."

This was nonsense, of course—pure wistful thinking. As the Great Depression lifted and the economy began to pick up under the stimulus of an approaching war, the Federal Arts projects became superfluous and politically embarrassing. The Federal Theatre was liquidated, buried and largely forgotten in the new excitement of World War II. Looking back sadly on my own accomplishment as head of New York's Negro Theatre, I felt that little of lasting value had been accomplished. "Negro playwrights were not appreciably encouraged or stimulated by our efforts and Negro actors (with a few notable exceptions) were held, for another twenty years, within the galling bounds of stereotyped roles. The black technicians we had developed were once again excluded from every professional theatrical union throughout the country. No black company came into existence and, for the next twenty years, no Negro audiences clamored for a continuation of the entertainment they had appeared to enjoy under the auspices of the WPA."

But in the long view I was wrong. We do, today, have black theatre; segregation has been drastically reduced in the theatre unions; black actors have generally escaped from their offensive stereotypes. And, over the country, dozens of regional theatres of various kinds thrive and multiply with programs that are more than vaguely reminiscent of the Federal Theatre. Above all, it is now generally recognized that government subsidy is a social and cultural necessity. Has the memory of the Federal Theatre played any part in all of this?

History works in mysterious ways: like bulbs that seem quite dead in the fall and amaze us with their blooms in the spring—it may be that our current theatrical renaissance can, in part, trace its origin to Hallie Flanagan's Federal Theatre—not so much to the actual structure that Congress condemned and dismantled in 1939 as to the spirit that animated it, the hope it offered, and the creative energy that it so miraculously generated. Vivid examples of that spirit and energy can be found in the pictures, memories, and original material contained in this beautiful and valuable book.

JOHN HOUSEMAN, *April 1978*

C O N T E N T S

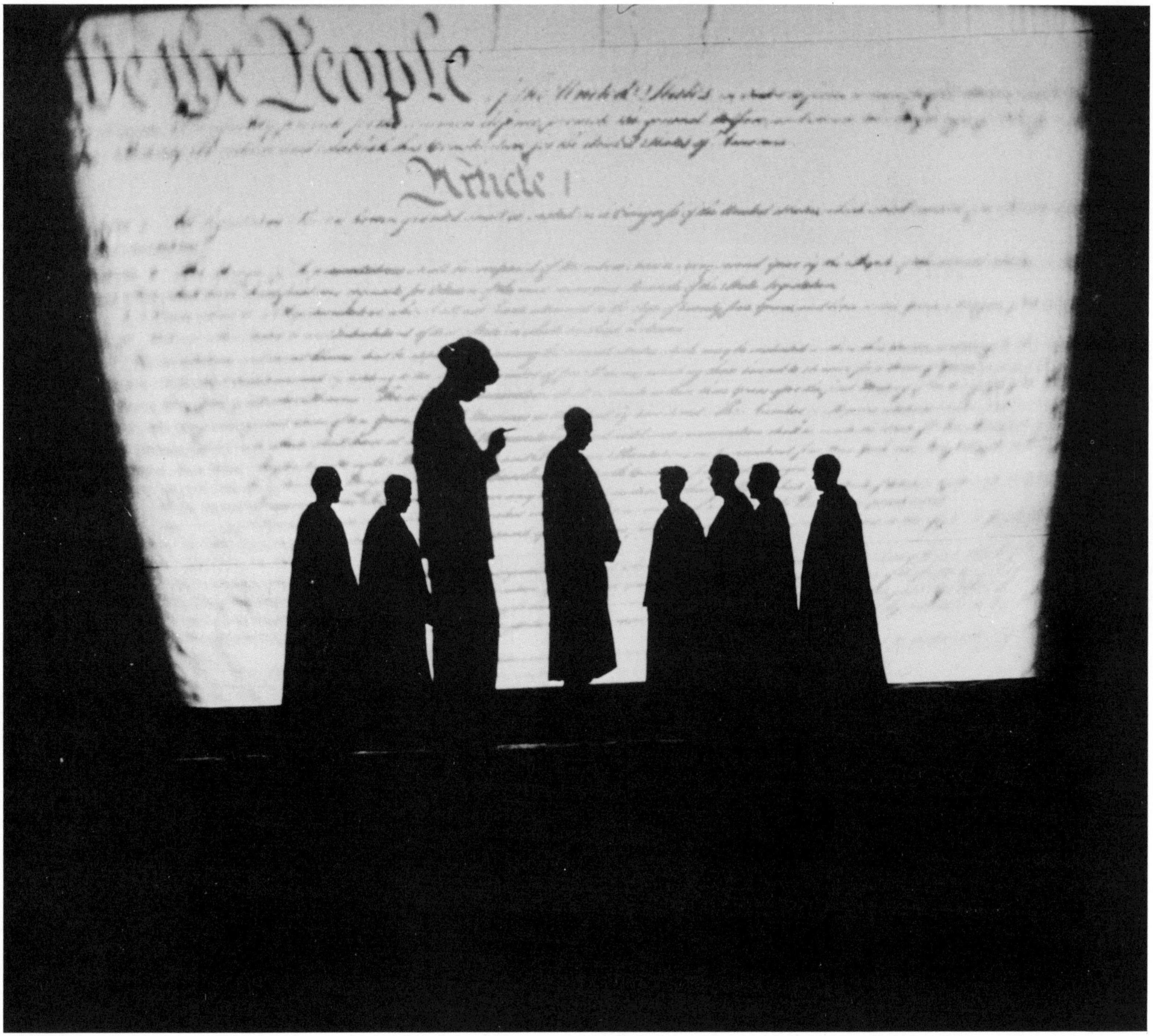
We the People
Article 1

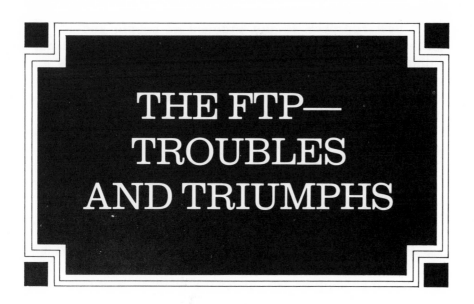

THE FTP— TROUBLES AND TRIUMPHS

THE PEOPLE

O F ALL THE ARTISTS to experience the effects of the Depression, the worst off were the show people. Unable to compete with the motion picture industry, actors, stagehands, technicians, musicians, and vaudeville performers found themselves displaced by technology even before the Crash. Sound films replaced the orchestra; mechanical music replaced musicians; actors were eclipsed by the Hollywood star system; and stagehands and stage mechanics were no longer needed. The impact of radio and a change in public taste added to the plight of those who were often thought of as "a dispensable luxury." Professional theatre people were stranded without work in major cities all over the country.

In the worsening economic climate of the thirties, as the numbers of unemployed increased in general, the theatre people also found themselves competing with unskilled laborers for manual jobs. Character actors who once had to play working men convincingly to capture a role, now had to dig the better ditch or saw more wood to win a job. Like other skilled but unemployed workers, theatre professionals were eligible for help from volunteer organizations and state and federal relief programs, but with that aid came the stigma and humiliation of being on the dole.

The Works Progress Administration, organized by Congress on April 8, 1935,

Eleanor Roosevelt, Harry Hopkins, and Fiorello LaGuardia.

indicated a new approach to the problem of people and of work. Only "employables"—healthy, unhandicapped persons—were to be taken from relief rolls of the states and offered work within their own skills and trades. "Unemployables"—people who could not and should not work—were to be returned to the care of the states. For the first time the skills of the worker and his self-respect became the cornerstone of a relief program.

Relief Administrator Harry Hopkins insisted that workers in the arts— painters, musicians, writers, actors, and other artists—were as deserving of support as workers with other skills. Within three months the Federal Theatre Project emerged as part of a white-collar division of the WPA, along with the Federal Music Project, Federal Art Project, and Federal Writers' Project. Together they employed forty thousand artists by the end of 1935, who produced a standard of work that was remarkably high and serious. Hopkins had helped to guarantee it by choosing dedicated and visionary directors for each project.

It was at the National Theatre Conference at the University of Iowa in the summer of 1935 that Hopkins announced the creation of a "free, adult, uncensored" federal theatre; he knew the forty-five-year-old woman accompanying him was just the person to make his vision come true. He told her: "This is a noncommercial theatre. It's got to be run by a person who sees right from the start that the profits won't be money profits. It's got to be run by a person who isn't interested just in the commercial type of show. I know something about the plays you've been doing for ten years, plays about American life. This is an American job, not just a New York job. I want someone who knows and cares about other parts of the country. It's a job just down your alley."

Hallie Flanagan had been a classmate of Hopkins' at Grinnell College in Iowa, but they probably never expected their paths to cross again. She had not planned on a career when she graduated, but sudden widowhood in 1919 forced her to support herself and her two small children. She taught high school for a year, then convinced her alma mater to hire her as an instructor of drama. There she distinguished herself quickly by writing a short play, which earned her an invitation to join George Pierce Baker's '47 Workshop, the foremost theatre laboratory in the nation. Flanagan went on to create an experimental theatre, first at Grinnell, then at Vassar. In 1926 she was the first woman to be awarded a Guggenheim fellowship, which she used to study European and Russian theatre. The year abroad was telling. On her return, her Vassar theatre began to earn a substantial reputation for its experimentation. Alistair Cooke compared it "with some of the most distinguished experimental theatres in Europe." Flanagan also wrote and produced *Can You Hear Their Voices?* an adaptation of a Whitaker Chambers' description of the Arkansas drought. In seven short scenes, the play dramatized the disparity in living conditions between rich and poor and the insensitivity of Congress. It was reviewed by the major newspapers and journals around the country, and colleges and little theatres across the nation clamored to produce it.

Despite Flanagan's success, the bosses of Broadway were skeptical of her appointment as Director of the Federal Theatre Project. They were not interested in her experimentation or her dream of a national federation of regional theatres. To them she was an amateur from a ritzy girl's school who knew little of the professionalism or hard commercialism of Broadway. The petite, red-haired woman would need her determination, as well as the encouragement of whatever connections she had—most notably, the help of Eleanor Roosevelt. As Harry Hopkins had told Flanagan on that trip to Iowa, "Don't forget that whatever happens you'll be wrong."

The first tough decision was who could be hired by the FTP. Some unions had dissuaded, even forbidden, members from enrolling in relief programs. Others insisted that all nonprofessionals be excluded from the Project and replaced by people of the highest professional rating. Lists were compiled that required even watchmen, elevator operators, janitors, typists, and truck drivers to have theatrical experience to be eligible for employment. In October 1935, Hallie Flanagan announced that hiring would be restricted to professional theatre people who had hitherto made their living in theatrical professions and who would be skilled enough to be able to make a living in the theatre at a later time. This restriction meant, for example, that graduates of university dramatic courses who were ready to return home and help in the establishment of theatre units could not participate in the Federal Theatre. It was a blow to the concept of truly regional theatre. Amateurs, no matter how talented, could not be employed unless they had enjoyed at least one professional engagement.

There was one exception: 10 percent of the employees did not have to be on relief. These people were supposed to be primarily supervisory. The heads of college theatres or little theatres, like Gilmor Brown of the Pasadena Playhouse or Jasper Deeter of the Hedgerow Theatre in Pennsylvania, were to provide the expert guidance necessary for the units to organize and begin to function across the nation. The 10 percent quota was also a way of attracting some inventive directors, like Joe Losey for the living newspapers or Elia Kazan for the New York City children's unit, who could handle the large casts of actors of varying ability. Occasionally tensions arose between the relief and nonrelief personnel, who often considered themselves a different breed: They had chosen to be on the Project. The tension was aggravated when the quota was almost immediately exceeded, and much to the embarrassment of the directors, most of the projects had to be allowed a 25 percent quota by January of 1936. When reductions were ordered later that year, however, the nonrelief workers were supposed to be cut first.

The question of who was a "professional," and the conflict between relief and

THE DIVISION OF WOMENS AND PROFESSIONAL PROJECTS OF THE WORKS PROGRESS ADMINISTRATION

PRESENTS

AN EXHIBITION

OF THE SKILLS OF THE UNEMPLOYED ON NON-MANUAL PROJECTS

NATIONAL MUSEUM

10th STREET & CONSTITUTION AVENUE, N.W.
WASHINGTON D.C.

JANUARY 10th to 31st

WEEKDAYS 9:30 A.M. TO 4:30 P.M.
SUNDAYS 1:30 P.M. TO 4:30 P.M.

The seamstress shop for the Lafayette unit.

nonrelief workers, were symptoms of the larger problem that would haunt the FTP until the end. Hallie Flanagan and her key assistants dreamed of creating a continuing national theatre out of the theatre relief project. According to Emmet Lavery, playwright, lawyer, and head of the National Service Bureau of the FTP, "If Federal Theatre could have survived for six months more, the second emergency, the actuality of war in Europe, would have perhaps extended the base of the first theatre operation. . . . This start on theatre, which was justified by the first emergency—the necessity of feeding hungry actors—could be held together on a more limited but very professional basis as a necessary arm of entertainment with the army. And if that had happened, we would have the national theatre." But a good national theatre needed talented, aggressive professionals—bright new workers who were willing to experiment and gamble—just the people who could find employment in the commercial theatre and who could not qualify for this relief project. Senator Josiah W. Bailey of North Carolina stated the problem explicitly: "The object of the WPA is to relieve distress and prevent suffering by providing work. The purpose is not the culture of the population." That the FTP did provide relief as well as attend to the "culture of the population" is an indication of the drive and determination not only of Hallie Flanagan, but of many of the FTP's workers.

Flanagan broadened the Project in every possible way, encouraging vaudeville, variety, and circus productions and insisting that educational projects be a part of every unit. Marionette and children's theatre companies were organized. Theatrical companies were developed to tour Civilian Conservation Corps (CCC) camps, and places where there had been no theatre previously. Her vision was to bring together old and young artists working in an apprentice-master relationship. The older artist could offer experience and advice; the younger would contribute new ideas and vitality to the partnership. Together they would bring theatre—in all its forms—to people who had never seen it, and whose lives desperately needed it.

Federal Theatre welcomed back the old stock stars of pre-Depression days. The thirties audience recognized and applauded such actors as Ian Maclaren, formerly of the Theatre Guild, and Alexander Carr, who played his old role in the Federal Theatre's revival of *Potash and Perlmutter*. People flocked to see actors like those two and like Oscar O'Shea, who was credited with keeping Martin Flavin's *Broken Dishes* running for seventeen weeks in the heat of a Chicago summer. Other old actors were retrained for the children's theatre, living newspapers, and musical reviews. Many quite predictably waited in the FTP green rooms rehearsing their roles, reading the newspapers, and reliving the past.

For the young, the FTP presented a chance to learn and experiment. Today's theatre is enriched and strengthened by many of the actors—people like Arthur

Kennedy, John Huston, E. G. Marshall and Johnny Randolph—who received early training and recognition in the Federal Theatre. Young playwrights like Oscar Saul and Herb Meadow, and directors like Vincent Sherman found permanent homes in Hollywood after developing their craft in the Federal Theatre. Sometimes the FTP job did not always indicate the future career: playwrights Arthur Miller, Norman Rosten, and Arnold Sundgaard read and evaluated plays by other authors; Dale Wasserman (author of *Man of La Mancha* and the screenplay of *One Flew Over the Cuckoo's Nest)*, and Nick Ray (author and director of *Rebel Without a Cause*, among other movies) were stage managers. Sidney Lumet was a child actor.

John Houseman and Orson Welles, themselves examples of the FTP's opportunities for new faces, filled their unit with actors and actresses who shared their energy and excitement: Joseph Cotten, Howard da Silva, Arlene Francis, Will Geer, Paula Laurence, Canada Lee, Hiram Sherman, Jack Carter, and Edna Thomas. They were joined by composer Virgil Thomson, lighting designer Abe Feder (who continues to try to light the world, or at least such parts as the Rockefeller Center, the Kennedy Center, and the U.N. Building), and publicity agent Allan Meltzer (who took the techniques he learned with the FTP to his subsequent career as publicity agent for Warner Brothers). Tragically, some of the brightest young stars of the Federal Theatre, who would surely have become famous, died within a few years after the Project closed—actor Erford Gage, directors Lem Ward and Yasha Frank, and designer Nat Karson.

Will Lee in *The Miser*. New York City.

Some of the greatest opportunities for the young were behind the scenes. The experience of George Izenour, though not entirely typical, was a good example of the possibilities the FTP represented. He joined the Los Angeles unit on the strength of his physics M. A. thesis and a fifteen-minute interview with Hallie Flanagan, who happened to be passing through town. Between November 1937 and December 1938, he was supervisor of lighting for all seven Los Angeles theatres and worked on more than 150 productions. Called the "Moscow lighting director" by the older and more experienced stage hands because of his "foreign" notions of how a play could be lit, Izenour chose as his supervisor of electricians a seventy-year-old veteran to act as his go-between with the men—a perfect example of the link between old and young that characterized the FTP. Because of his success in Los Angeles, Izenour was selected to light the FTP theatre being constructed as part of the San Francisco Exposition. He seized the opportunity to develop a board that would electronically control all of the dimmers. This led to a Rockefeller Foundation grant and a professorship at Yale, where he was able to perfect his "console," an electronic dimmer that revolutionized the lighting of modern stage shows.

Similar stories can be told about FTP set and costume designers like Howard Bay, Ben Edwards, Charles Elson, Kate Drain Lawson, Fred Stover, and Sam

Lighting console designed by George Izenour.

Ben Edwards' set for *Pygmalion*. Roslyn, New York.

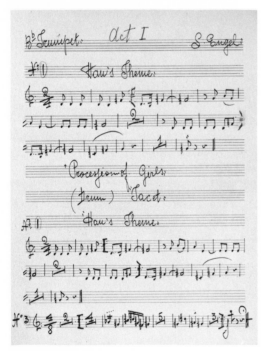

Lehman Engel's score for *The Emperor's New Clothes*.

Leve, who were able to find numerous design jobs after their work in the Federal Theatre. They became the major designers for the generation after World War II. Some, like Stover and Lawson, went into films or television; others, like Bay (who designed many of the great musicals of the fifties and sixties), and Elson (editor of the two-volume *Design Throughout the World*) eventually went into teaching, though they continue to design for Broadway shows. Edwards, who worked with the Roslyn, Long Island, FTP unit, has been particularly busy recently with O'Neill revivals like *Anna Christie* and *A Touch of the Poet* and all three plays in *The Texas Trilogy*. Together, all of them firmly established stage design as a significant artistic profession.

For some of the young people, working for the FTP could have its ironies. Lehman Engel, who was just beginning to have a reputation in music, found his talents eagerly sought after by the Project. Commissioned to do incidental music for *The Emperor's New Clothes,* Engel's contract called for a three dollar royalty every time the music was played. Given the popularity of the children's show and the fact that the music was composed in two and a half hours, Engel's royalties of three thousand dollars was some of the easiest money he had ever made.

Perhaps the real measure of the Federal Theatre should not be the now-famous names, but rather the thousands of unknown people in rural towns, CCC camps, and city parks who saw live theatre for the first time, and the hundreds of people who had given their lives to the theatre, who were able to end or continue their careers with pride, doing what they were trained to do and did well.

THE PRODUCTIONS

IN HINDSIGHT the value of the Federal Theatre Project is obvious, but in the spring of 1936 the FTP was in desperate need of some hits in order to prove its worth. After months of dealing with the red tape of setting up a government relief program and the potentially paralyzing scandal of the censorship of its first major Broadway production of a new play *(Ethiopia),* the FTP needed a boost in morale, evidence that the whole idea of federally sponsored theatre would be worthwhile. During March and April of that year, the New York units opened four plays that quickly established the FTP's identity and assured its success. The productions of *Triple-A Plowed Under,* the first produced living newspaper; *Murder in the Cathedral,* the world premiere of T. S. Eliot's verse drama about Thomas à Becket; *Chalk Dust,* an attack on America's educational system; and the "voodoo" *Macbeth,* Orson Welles' Negro adaptation, forcefully demonstrated the Federal Theatre's willingness to take chances in its selection of plays and to experiment in its productions. More importantly, they demonstrated that there was a place for a national theatre that would mount plays that other theatrical organizations—whether commercial producers of Broadway or the committed little theatres—would not.

Despite its being foremost a relief agency, the Federal Theatre had several advantages over other producing organizations. First, it was not tied to the box office. Thus it could take greater risks in play selection than the commercial theatre. *Murder in the Cathedral,* for instance, had been rejected by the Theatre Guild, which had been offering serious drama since 1919.

Second, it could provide a stability that the little theatres could rarely afford. Many of the people who had participated in such workers' groups as the Theatre of Action or the Theatre Collective joined the Federal Theatre, where they could count on a regular paycheck. They also hoped that the FTP would produce, on a grander scale, the plays they would like to have done when they were a workers' theatre. When the leftist Theatre Union dissolved (partly because it was competing for the same audience as the FTP), the Federal Theatre took over its next planned production, *Life and Death of an American.*

Third, the Federal Theatre could employ larger casts and take longer time in rehearsal than other theatre groups. Three of the four FTP hits in the spring of 1936 had casts of nearly 100 actors, plus scores of technicians and stage hands. Playwrights could write for the FTP without regard to the size of the cast. Multi-scene reviews like *Sing for Your Supper*, or the epic living newspapers, were done almost exclusively by the Project.

Finally, because 90 percent of the money allotted to FTP had to be spent on salaries, the groups had to develop specialized settings and stagecraft. Money went into lights, which could be used in one play after another, rather than sets and props that had a more limited life span. Though there were notable exceptions, designers and lighting experts moved away from lavish sets and developed settings that relied on abstract space and symbolic realism. Eliot's *Murder in the Cathedral* offers a good example of necessity turned to advantage.

The play's poetic qualities had to be transformed into dramatic energies. The plot was essentially focused on one man and, even with Harry Irvine as the Archbishop, the limited action needed the support of some striking visual images. Aline Bernstein was to design the set, but as the opening date neared, director Halsted Welles, who taught at the Yale Drama School, was forced to improvise. He used a minimum of stark props to suggest the scene, a row of spear bearers, and a pale cyclorama. The resulting depth and expansiveness of the stage could also turn ominously constricted through sudden changes in lighting.

At the heart of this stage design was an abstract quality that widened the

Federal Theatre was a wonderful, lucky thing because it kept alive possibilities in people who would never have made it otherwise, who would never have ended up in theatre at all. I myself might be one of them—I'm not absolutely sure. I was getting along barely; but living on about ten dollars a week while trying to practice one's art, you may not survive too long. So Federal Theatre gave me two excellent opportunities. One was to stay alive, which was rather nice, and the other was a chance to learn arts that I didn't know, that I was primitively ignorant about. . . . It was very important for me and it was fortuitous, a beautiful piece of luck when it happened.

DALE WASSERMAN, *playwright*

Murder in the Cathedral. New York City.

scope of action and mood and gave the play a timelessness and universality. Such design created the atmosphere of a scene with the greatest simplicity. Although the technique could be used in realistic plays, it always opposed "copying on the stage the confusion and detail of actuality." Space staging, in contrast to the theatre of photographic realism, encouraged stylization.

The response to the production was tremendous; during the six-week run over thirty-nine thousand people saw the show. *Billboard* described one reception of the play: "a hard-boiled audience of Broadway professionals stood up and cheered, literally stood and cheered as this reporter has seldom if ever heard an audience cheer in the theatre." A year later when an English company toured with their production of *Murder in the Cathedral* in New York and Boston, the critics thought it did not match the Federal Theatre production's "intensity" or "intelligence." Halsted Welles had joined the FTP only for this production, but he was so impressed by the possibilities of a national theatre that he stayed to head the newly formed test unit, which tried out scripts by the FTP's own developing playwrights, who included Howard Koch, Arthur Miller, Norman Rosten, and Arnold Sundgaard.

A different Welles (no relation) was responsible, with John Houseman, for another of the spring surprises, the "voodoo" *Macbeth*. With Rose McClendon, Houseman had been appointed codirector of the New York City Negro unit, because of his friendship with McClendon. He asked the young, brilliant Orson Welles, who had just toured with Katherine Cornell in *Romeo and Juliet,* to direct *Macbeth*. They decided on that play in part because the Negro actors wanted to prove that they could successfully perform the classics, that they could "discard the bandanna and burnt cork casting to play a universal character," and in part because Elizabethan drama was well suited to Welles' energy and theatricality.

The setting of the play was changed to Haiti, and designer Nat Karson created a fantastic set of a high-walled castle in the midst of a Caribbean jungle. The musical score, composed by Virgil Thomson, was filled with voodoo drums and the piercing cries of a coven of witches. Welles took advantage of an African dance group that was stranded in New York, and a practicing African witch doctor to create a mood of frenzied evil. Brooks Atkinson described the effect of the witches in his review:

> *The witches have always worried the life out of the polite tragic stage. . . . But ship the witches down into the rank and fever-stricken jungle of Haiti, dress them in fantastic costumes, crowd the stage with mad and gabbing throngs of evil worshippers, beat the jungle drums, raise the voices until the jungle echoes, stuff a gleaming naked witch doctor into the cauldron, hold up Negro masks in the baleful light—and there you have a witches' scene that is logical and stunning and a triumph of theatre art.*

The spectacle brought the Broadway patrons and critics to Harlem in droves. After a seven-month New York run, the play went on a nationwide tour.

Though the production was dominated by Welles' vision, he worked with some talented actors. Macbeth and his lady were played by Jack Carter and Edna Thomas. Canada Lee played Banquo, and Eric Burroughs, the sinister Hecate. The Lafayette Theatre in Harlem was now established, and the black unit would continue to produce a series of hits for the FTP. The success of *Macbeth* also encouraged Negro units across the country to adapt previously "white-only" plays, from Aristophanes' *Lysistrata* in Seattle, to Gilbert and Sullivan's *Mikado* in Chicago.

With *Chalk Dust,* by Harold Clarke and Maxwell Nurnberg, the Federal Theatre announced its commitment to produce new, socially relevant drama. The play attacked the bureaucracy and intolerance of the public school system by portraying the daily life of teachers in a metropolitan high school. *Chalk Dust* was a typical "social drama" of the thirties with its realistic setting, sympathetic protagonist (a young teacher battling the system), romantic interludes, and a cautiously upbeat ending. The FTP even organized an advisory board of educators, featuring John Dewey and Roger Baldwin, to promote the play and insure against attacks on the play's authenticity or value. The plan worked so well that the Project adopted it for other socially conscious productions like *One-Third of a Nation* and *Spirochete.*

As it did with the other major spring successes, the Federal Theatre assigned some of its best talent to the New York production of *Chalk Dust.* The staff was a good example of how the FTP brought older, well-established theatre people together with younger artists hoping to remain in the profession during the Depression. Virgil Geddes, author of *Native Ground,* produced the play with the help of Vincent Sherman, who went on to direct *It Can't Happen Here* and numerous Hollywood films. James Light, the director, had earned his reputation a decade earlier at the Provincetown Playhouse, where he had brought to life Eugene O'Neill's plays, including *Beyond the Horizon, Hairy Ape,* and *Emperor Jones.* Howard Bay did the sets.

Chalk Dust ran for two months in New York, and productions were subsequently mounted in ten other cities. This show set an FTP pattern: a New York opening followed by productions around the country. The later productions benefited from the New York director's report, the designs, the lighting and sound plots, and the critics' reviews.

 MORE FORCEFUL example of the FTP's desire to produce plays on controversial topics was the spring's fourth and most significant hit, *Triple-A Plowed Under,* a living newspaper about agriculture.

Jack Carter and Edna Thomas in *Macbeth.* New York City.

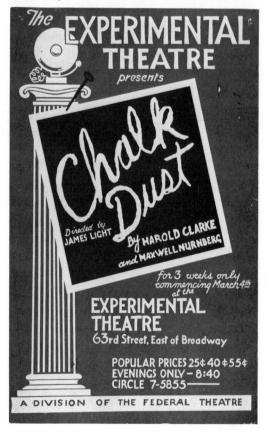

The EXPERIMENTAL THEATRE presents *Chalk Dust*

Directed by JAMES LIGHT

By HAROLD CLARKE and MAXWELL NURNBERG

for 3 weeks only commencing March 4th at the

EXPERIMENTAL THEATRE
63rd Street, East of Broadway

POPULAR PRICES 25¢ 40¢ 55¢
EVENINGS ONLY – 8:40
CIRCLE 7-5855

A DIVISION OF THE FEDERAL THEATRE

The living newspaper was a new dramatic form—a committed documentary that informed the audience of the size, nature, and origin of a social problem, and then called for specific action to solve it. Various people (including Hallie Flanagan, Elmer Rice, and Morris Watson, a cofounder of the Newspaper Guild) are credited with the idea, which brought together both unemployed newspaper men and theatre personnel.

The living newspaper unit in New York had tried to produce a living newspaper on the Ethiopian war, but that had been canceled by the White House (*See* pp. 26-27.) *Triple-A Plowed Under* was the second attempt, and despite the actors' doubts during rehearsals that it really wasn't a play, it was a tremendous critical and popular success. The New York production, directed by Joe Losey and H. Gordon Graham, with music by Lee Wainer, ran for eighty-five performances and the play was later produced in Chicago, Cleveland, Los Angeles, and Milwaukee.

Triple-A dramatized the need for the farmer and consumer to unite for better incomes and cheaper food. It relived some of the recent events that had affected farmers and farm prices—the milk strike of 1932, the Agriculture Adjustment Act's cutting of farm production, the greed of the grocer middleman—and examined two proposed solutions, the Soil Conservation Act and the Farmer-Labor party. The topic did not seem to be a likely one for New York audiences, but living newspaper techniques made it exciting as well as informative theatre.

Projections, masks, spotlights, loudspeakers, ramps, and characters in the audience were some of the devices used to force the facts upon the audience in an unforgettable fashion. The projections, still a new theatrical concept in America, could include such factual information as dates, statistics, charts, maps, and headlines, or they could be more visual: photographs, animated cartoons, and short film sequences. The images were projected onto a curtain, known as a scrim. Because it was translucent, shadows could also be thrown onto the scrim by strong lights at the back of the stage. *Triple-A* used both methods effectively; in one scene, shadows of various famous Americans, ranging from Thomas Jefferson to Earl Browder (the head of the American Communist party in the thirties), could be seen on the back of the scrim, while the Preamble to the Declaration of Independence was projected in front. The projections could provide a startling counterpoint to the action occurring downstage. They dramatically extended the stage space and forced the spectator to sit up in his seat in order to catch all that was happening about him.

Another assault on the traditionally passive spectator's senses was an offstage loudspeaker, occasionally called the "Voice of the Living Newspaper." Essentially an American creation, this was a transitional figure who introduced new characters, established time and place, and linked the episodes. On occasion the loudspeaker became the voice of the public, posing questions and pressuring officials, thus keeping the action lively and dramatic while sharing his knowledge with the audience. The loudspeaker could also convey street or crowd noises, or other noises of the industrial world, and amplify them to a hysterical pitch. In another famous scene in *Triple-A,* the loudspeaker announces, "Summer, 1934: Drought sears the Midwest, West, and Southwest," and repeats the weather report, "fair and warmer," for four successive days: May 1st, May 2nd. . . . Then a farmer on stage, who has been crouching down, stands up, "slowly lets a handful of dry dust sift through his fingers," and cries "Dust!" This fusion of factual information and theatrical symbol had a powerful emotional impact and was typical of the living newspaper's stagecraft.

Living newspapers were written on such varied topics as housing, health care, cooperatives, natural resources, labor unions, Negroes, the movies, and public utilities. Each play was thoroughly documented, but they did have an editorial slant: personal problems were caused by social conditions; the lack of housing, food, or electricity was the result of a private enterprise system that ex-

W.P.A. FEDERAL
THEATRE PROJECT
LIVING NEWSPAPER
PRESENTS

POWER

BY ARTHUR ARENT

RITZ
THEATRE
48th STREET
West of Broadway

FEDERAL ART PROJECT N.Y.C.

ploited human needs. Most of the plays ended with exhortations demanding specific legislative or judicial action.

The New York living newspaper unit was consciously communal in its creation of the script and production of the play. A number of newspaper men and writers would do the research and develop scenarios and drafts of the play. Arthur Arent, the editor-in-chief (head playwright), would then polish the script, making the most of juxtaposition, short scenes, and dramatic symbols. During rehearsal, the play would be modified further by the director and actors. As a group they would decide on props and hand settings. The portable setting made possible both the precision and rapid pace necessary for expository scenes. The actors generally did not have strongly individualized parts; rather, they moved and often spoke in groups.

The New York living newspaper unit went on during the next two years to produce *1935*, a review of the events of the year; *Injunction Granted*, a history of labor unions in the courts; *Power*, a call for public ownership of utilities; and *One-Third of a Nation*, an exposé of housing conditions in the big cities. The living newspaper form probably reached its full maturity with *Power*, which opened in February 1937 and ran for five months. It was also produced in Chicago, Portland, San Francisco, and Seattle, where the mayor declared "*Power* Week."

The concept of a dramatic presentation of a problem (the play opens with a power failure), coupled with the historical explanation of its causes and an examination of possible solutions, is more effectively brought to life here than in the other plays. The tighter structure was primarily due to the interweaving of documentary facts with fictional scenes or characters, which included an everyman figure. Angus K. Buttonkooper, played by Norman Lloyd in the New York production, is a "meek-looking" consumer who is ignorant of the whys and hows of electricity, but knows his electric bill is too high. He appears in five of the play's twenty-one scenes, asking questions, getting confused, and becoming increasingly angry. In the process of his education, the audience learns both about the technical aspects of electricity and the monopolistic business practices of the power industry. Unlike his portrayal in most social dramas of the period, however, this sympathetic little man remains ineffective.

At the end of the first act the government intervenes and the Tennessee Valley Authority (TVA) is established. The second act (*Power* was the first living newspaper to have two acts) begins with the workers and farmers, singing in front of a projection of waterfalls and power dams:

> All up and down the valley
> They heard the glad alarm
> The Government means business—
> It's working like a charm.

*Oh, see them boys a-comin
Their Government they trust.*

Most of the second act explains the need for the TVA and why there is opposition to it. The final curtain comes down with a question mark on it, as the loudspeaker asks, "What will the Supreme Court do?"

This strong support of a New Deal project was greatly appreciated by Harry Hopkins, who came backstage to tell the cast that,

> *It's fast and funny, it makes you laugh and it makes you cry and it makes you think—I don't know what more anyone can ask of a show. I want this play and plays like it done from one end of the country to the other . . . . Now let's get one thing clear: you will take a lot of criticism on this play. People will say it's propaganda. Well, I say what of it? It's propaganda to educate the consumer who's paying for power. It's about time someone had some propaganda for him. The big power companies have spent millions on propaganda for the utilities. It's about time that the consumer had a mouthpiece. I say more plays like* Power *and more power to you.*

With its popular (over sixty thousand advance ticket sales) and relatively uncontroversial success, *Power* became a model for living newspapers written by individuals and FTP units across the country. In Chicago, the local unit produced Arnold Sundgaard's *Spirochete,* a living newspaper about the history of syphilis. Sundgaard wrote the play in 1938 in response to a national "war on syphilis" headed by the surgeon general.

In typical living newspaper fashion, *Spirochete* reviews the history of the problem—its origins, its rapid spread through Europe, its cost in "human terms"—and urges the passage of mandatory blood tests for marriage licenses. Sundgaard modified the everyman figure into an "eternal patient," who wanders through the play in search of a cure for his dread disease. With the enthusiastic support of local health agencies, it was also produced in Philadelphia, Portland, Seattle, Boston, and Cincinnati. Other openings were planned, and then subsequently canceled when the FTP closed.

The plight of the underprivileged (or even the common man) under industrial capitalism, and the conflict between preserving natural resources and industry's need for raw material and cheap labor, were favorite topics for many living newspaper authors. *Spanish Grant,* by Eugene Deaderick and *Land Grant,* by T. C. Robinson and Rena Vale (both about private property in Southern California), *Poor Little Consumer,* by Robert Russell (the need for a consumer's union), and *Townsend Goes to Town,* by George Murray and David Peltz (an alternative to social security), all show big business interests consistently in conflict with the safety and well-being of the powerless individual. Similarly,

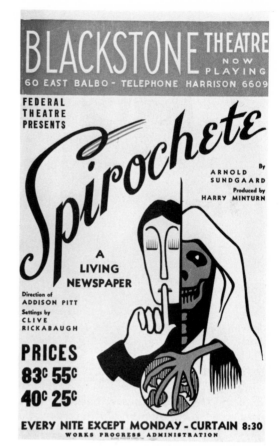

BLACKSTONE THEATRE
NOW PLAYING
60 EAST BALBO - TELEPHONE HARRISON 6609

FEDERAL THEATRE PRESENTS

Spirochete

By ARNOLD SUNDGAARD

Produced by HARRY MINTURN

A LIVING NEWSPAPER

Direction of ADDISON PITT
Settings by CLIVE RICKABAUGH

PRICES 83¢ 55¢ 40¢ 25¢

EVERY NITE EXCEPT MONDAY - CURTAIN 8:30
WORKS PROGRESS ADMINISTRATION

Joseph Lentz designed the set for *Altars of Steel*. Atlanta.

Dirt, by Don Farran and Ruth Stewart (agribusiness in Iowa), *Timber,* by Burke Ormsby and Mary Myrtle (the lumber industry in Washington state), *Tapestry in Linen* (the flax industry in Oregon), and *King Cotton,* by Betty Smith and Robert Finch (cotton and the textile mills in the South), reveal how a region's resources are depleted and the small farmer is driven out by giant businesses that own both the land and the industry—from lumber in the North to textiles in the South.

Though each region was encouraged to develop living newspapers on local problems, few were produced. The national office of the FTP wanted full documentation and proof that they were factually accurate. Fictionalized social drama based on regional problems were more easily approved. *Altars of Steel,* by southerner Thomas Hall-Rogers, dramatized the effects of absentee ownership, labor organizing, and ruthless price cutting in the growing southern steel industry. In the play a small, southern mill is bought by United Steel and immediately, both labor and capital seek unfair advantage over each other. The two major characters—the former mill owner and a labor organizer—die during a riot at the plant, and nineteen workers die in an open-hearth explosion. The play caused a tremendous controversy in Atlanta where it opened, possibly because the author was so evenhanded in his depiction of the conflict. Columnists used the play as a focal point in blaming or praising the changes in society in general.

T HE POWER of the "well-aimed fact" that made the living newspapers so effective was also behind the popularity of history plays. Even when some of the characters or events were fictional, history plays were based on facts, and "real" experience was prized in the thirties. The actual, rather than the imagined, was the path to truth. Writers searched the American past for ideals that had been forgotten, and people and events that could serve as models during the Depression. The quest was also reflected in various other WPA arts projects. The Writers' Project guide books, the folk song collections, the Index of American Design, the slave narratives, and the Historical Records Survey were some of the ways that the government tried to preserve and promote the American heritage.

The history play was not restricted, however, to a simple celebration of the American spirit overcoming adversity. Playwrights—from the classical Greeks, to the Elizabethans and more recently, George Bernard Shaw—had traditionally written about particular moments in the past to make a point about the present. The FTP was no exception. For example, *Created Equal* by John Hunter Booth, examined the conflict between the actions of the propertied class and the civil and personal rights of all people throughout American history. Booth started with the landing of the Mayflower and traced the history of the Constitution through Philip Schuyler and his descendants. They were joined by a chorus that acted as the enraged citizens of the Boston Tea Party, the hardy pioneers of the wagon trains, and other groups at key historical moments.

First produced in Boston in May 1938, with much fanfare and wide community support, the play was subsequently staged in Springfield, Massachusetts, and Newark, New Jersey. A reporter from *Billboard* wrote, "every American should be shown this theatrical document. . . . It is better than twenty-five years of dull history courses." Not everyone agreed, however, that *Created Equal* was good American history. Half of the cast in the Newark production signed a petition declaring the play "un-American." Although their complaint was not taken seriously (they also objected to *Triple-A* and *It Can't Happen Here),* the striking contrast between the *Billboard* reporter and the New Jersey cast points out that the telling of history was seen as a significant political act.

In *Battle Hymn,* which followed *Chalk Dust* at the New York experimental theatre, Michael Gold and Michael Blankfort chose abolitionist John Brown as a symbol of the necessity of violence to create change. Brown, a Christian and a pacifist, began as a Kansas farmer, but when the slavery war in that state took the life of his son, he became an impassioned abolitionist. Finally, Brown turned to violence in order to stop an unjust law and overthrow a social order based on slavery. Reviewers in both New York and San Francisco, amid their praise, pointed to contemporary parallels. Given some of Brown's speeches (written by Blankfort and Gold), Howard Bay's set design, and the forceful direction of Vincent Sherman, it is surprising that this play escaped congressional notice.

Federal Theatre plays about other important historical figures or popular heroes included *Lucy Stone* by Maud Wood Park, *Jefferson Davis* by John McGee, *Ballad of Davy Crockett* by Hoffman Hays, *Everywhere I Roam* (about Johnny Appleseed) by Arnold Sundgaard, *Booker T. Washington* by Abram Hill, and *John Henry* by Frank Wells. (Ted Browne's *Natural Man* was also about John Henry.)

The most popular historical stage figure was Abe Lincoln. Two plays were simply titled *Abraham Lincoln*—one by Ralph Kettering and one by John Drinkwater. *Mrs. Lincoln* by Ramon Romero, and *The Lonely Man* by Howard Koch, were variations on the theme. *Prologue to Glory,* by E. P. Conkle, with its twenty-plus productions, was the climax of American history as presented by the FTP. Conkle's play focused on Lincoln's love for Ann Rutledge as his early and lasting inspiration. Separate productions toured in all regions of the country and were seen by hundreds of thousands of theatre-goers. The play ran for eleven months in New York City and then moved to the World's Fair. The New York production was a press agent's dream: the actress playing Ann Rutledge was named Ann Rutledge, and was the great-grandniece of Lincoln's sweetheart. In New York, Lincoln was played by one of the FTP's finest young actors, Erford Gage. This production earned the strong praise of Burns Mantle, who listed it as

Projection for *Created Equal*. Boston.

John Huston in *Lonely Man*. Chicago.

Ann Rutledge in *Prologue to Glory*. New York City.

one of the ten best productions of 1938: "If the Federal Theatre had produced no other single drama, this production of *Prologue to Glory* would doubly justify its history and all its struggles."

As with *Created Equal,* not everyone agreed about the value or purpose of *Prologue to Glory.* Congressman J. Parnell Thomas objected to Lincoln's speech in the play that "subjects for debate before the forum ought to be alive—subjects for action, useful in living." Thomas claimed it was "Communist talk," and found *Prologue to Glory* "a propaganda play to prove that all politicians are crooked."

A specialized, blander variation was the pageant, a celebration of a local historical event often staged outdoors. Hallie Flanagan strongly encouraged them, as central to her regional theatre and people's theatre ideals. The most successful FTP pageant is still staged every summer at Manteo, North Carolina, in a WPA-built outdoor theatre. *The Lost Colony,* by Paul Green, recounts the story of Virginia Dare, the first Anglo-Saxon born in America, in the colony founded by Sir Walter Raleigh. The play, first produced in 1937, attracted many New York critics and Washington dignitaries; President and Mrs. Roosevelt also attended a performance. In 1938, Green and Kurt Weill were commissioned to write another pageant, *Our Common Glory,* but the FTP closed before it could be staged the next summer. Years later, Green modified the play for Colonial Williamsburg, where it is now shown annually.

At the opposite end of the nation, in Vancouver, Washington, a similar pageant reenacted the arrival of Americans to the Hudson Bay colony at Fort Vancouver. The *Flotilla of Faith* was performed on the Columbia River and its bluffs, where the original landing had occurred. The elaborate "re-production" involved canoes, local native Indian dancers, and a feast in which the spectators joined. Smaller pageants, often celebrating the founding of a community, were performed by FTP units in Florida, Massachusetts, Oklahoma, and California.

Flotilla of Faith. Vancouver, Washington.

A SPECIALIZED FORM of the history play took place on radio, where the major networks gave the Federal Theatre Radio Division over five million dollars of free air time (ten times the cost of the whole Radio Division). Over sixty radio series were heard from March 1936 to the FTP closing, an average of three thousand programs a year. Over one-fifth of these programs were histories, including such serials as *History in Action, Pioneers of Science, Portraits in Oil,* and *Once Upon a Time.* The broadcasts, generally originating in New York, lasted from fifteen minutes to an hour, and used scripts from a variety of sources: *Epic of America* was a fifteen-part dramatization from the book by James Truslow Adams; *Men Against Death* was based on Paul de Kruif's *Microbe Hunters.* Some fifteen-minute biographies of scientists and artists were written by Radio Division authors, while other serials, like Jane Ashman's *Women in the Making of America,* were rented.

Like the theatre units, the Radio Division was free of commercial constraints, and the staff experimented with both the content and style of their offerings. (Any of their technical innovations were then made available to all commercial broadcasters.) Besides the historical programs, FTP Radio offered educational shows on health, safety, and law, as well as adaptations of stage plays and short stories. Plays by Ibsen and Shakespeare and other examples of Elizabethan and contemporary theatre were adapted for radio. The Shakespeare series proved so popular that both NBC and CBS developed their own versions. Mary Roberts Rinehart's series, *Tish,* adapted for the FTP, became the most popular series on CBS in the spring 1938 season. It too was continued by the network after the FTP run. In fact, a number of both fiction and nonfiction programs, as well as 50 percent of the staff, continued with commercial radio after the close of the FTP. Thus, the Radio Division was particularly successful in meeting the Federal Theatre goals: producing quality shows that were a stimulating alter-

Swing Mikado. Chicago.

native to commercial fare, and training professionals who could return to private enterprise with new skills and experience.

THE SIXTEEN NEGRO UNITS of the Federal Theatre Project were scattered across America from Boston to Los Angeles, and Seattle to Atlanta, with a cluster of units in the northeast coast around Hartford, Buffalo, New York City, Newark, and Philadelphia. The largest unit was, of course, in New York, headquartered at the Lafayette Theatre where that talented and energetic group put on thirty productions between 1935 and 1939.

The productions of these units reflected a wide variety of dramatic material, ranging from adaptations of classics like *Macbeth, The Mikado,* and *Lysistrata* through African dance, musical reviews, minstrel shows, and vaudeville, to new works written for the FTP, such as Theodore Browne's *Go Down Moses,* Hughes Allison's *Panyared,* and Abram Hill and John Silvera's living newspaper, *Liberty Deferred.* The units did plays by Shaw and O'Neill. They produced works by European playwrights like Andre Obey's *Noah* and Andreev's *The Sabine Women.* They performed historical plays about Napoleon's fruitless attempts to recapture Haiti, and Toussaint, Christophe, and Dessalines came alive for many people who had never attended the theatre before.

If such eclecticism allowed directors, actors, and producers to show their versatility, it did not, as the critic Sterling Brown has pointed out, produce a body of plays comparable to the repertory of the Abbey or Yiddish Theatre, but then the FTP was short-lived and many playwrights didn't trust even a Federal Project to do what it promised until there was substantial proof that serious dramatic efforts would be judged on their merits.

At the Lafayette, as in most of the Negro units across the country, the director was white, emphasizing, it was said, the lack of Negroes with administrative, directorial, and technical experience; more importantly, a white person was needed to get the units the federal money they had coming to them. As Carlton Moss, later one of the directors of the Lafayette unit, observed, "You couldn't put a white man off an elevator in a downtown office building." Actress Rose McClendon, who before she fell ill was slated to be codirector of the Harlem unit, expressed the view at the inauguration of the project that Negroes had always been performers with little opportunity to learn direction, design, or even playwrighting, except by osmosis, so that she preferred to have them start under experienced direction. Certainly her choice of John Houseman as codirector, was a tribute to his administrative abilities and his skill at working with the folks downtown for the benefit of the Negro unit. Houseman was of European descent rather than a native-born American, and that added to his attractiveness and credibility with the unit, which some said he ran like a colonial governor.

When Houseman and Welles left the Harlem unit, Carlton Moss, Augustus Smith, and Harry Edward were put in charge. Moss was the "community man" who went to black lodges and churches to try to win new audiences for the unit. His goal was to create an environment where the community felt comfortable and would consider the theatre their own. The footprints painted on the sidewalk and the brass bands on the opening night of *Macbeth* at the Lafayette were products of this kind of community orientation and commitment. Gus Smith, no longer a young man when the Harlem unit burst into activity, directed, acted, and tried his hand at playwriting. In collaboration with Peter Morrell, he wrote *Turpentine,* which dramatized the plight of Negro workers in the Florida pine woods. Directing and starring in the leading role, he had the pleasure of a run of sixty-eight performances. Harry Edward was the administrator of the group and if his talents had been fully appreciated he could have become an invaluable member of Hallie Flanagan's staff.

Also vital to the success of the Lafayette unit was the work of Leonard de Paur who had been an assistant to Hall Johnson before the latter left New York for Los Angeles. Sought out by the FTP at Johnson's suggestion, de Paur worked with the Harlem unit from the beginning, arranging the music, directing the choir, and composing original scores. Obviously talented and creative, he then acted as musical consultant on other Federal Theatre shows.

The success of the Lafayette Theatre educated theatre people about the potential of skilled black workers and helped open the theatre professions to new groups. A young black stagehand like Henry Kinnard—who had been a stagehand in Harlem before the FTP and whose family had been stagehands before him—could finally join an auxiliary, and eventually work downtown. (Today Mr. Kinnard still works for NBC.) The Lafayette productions also gave Perry Watkins, the set designer, a chance to exhibit his artistry in such plays as *Haiti* and O'Neill's *S. S. Glencairn*, a trilogy of sea plays.

The Boston unit was a notable exception to white directorial control. There Ralf Coleman, who had been very active in Boston theatrical circles for many years as actor and director, wrote plays, acted, and directed, as well as managed a unit of over 150 people for the life of the project. He was aided in his efforts by Jack Bates, Ted Browne, and his brother, Warren Coleman. Another young man who had gone to Boston to study law visited the unit with a friend and stayed on for the four years: Frank Silvera, later one of the outstanding character actors in the American theatre, played in most of the unit's productions.

Rehearsals for all of the Boston units took place in Deacon Hall, where the close proximity of the units spurred competition, allowed the units to borrow actors, costumes, and scenery from each other, and made it possible to watch each other rehearse. From Coleman's point of view, these physical arrangements were ideal for developing the kind of excellence and commitment to the theatre

Gus Smith, left, and Louis Sharp, right, in *Turpentine*. New York City.

that his direction and influence had always fostered. One of their joint productions was *Created Equal* by John Hunter Booth.

An incident that testifies to the spirit and determination of the man and his unit involved their production of *Stevedore*. The play, by Paul Peter and George Sklar, told of a strong, courageous black man who dies defending himself against the white bosses and ended with black and white workers uniting. Inspired by accounts of Seattle's production in 1936, the Boston unit felt that the play would do especially well for them, but Federal Theatre officials disagreed. Coleman, not one to be easily discouraged, suggested that members of the unit rehearse the play on their own time and make ready for a non-Federal Theatre production elsewhere in the community. Officials, in a countermove, promptly scheduled a Federal Theatre performance for the group about thirty miles away in Salem, Massachusetts, on the same night as the scheduled opening of *Stevedore*. Ralf Coleman then arranged for the Salem engagement to begin at 7 p.m. Played without intermission, the performance was over in time for the cast, still in costume, to rush back to Boston where an audience, aware of the scheduling obstacles, had been waiting. As the performers arrived in the theatre, the audience rose to its feet and cheered. That night, *Stevedore* was enlivened by the joy, shared by audience and actors alike, of outwitting the would-be Federal Theatre censors.

The black unit in Chicago also faced problems of harassment and censorship by local officials when Paul Green's *Hymn to the Rising Sun* was closed. (*See* p. 29.) After their success with the jazz version of the medieval play, *Everyman,* such criticism came as a shock to the unit. It was several months before they were ready to face another audience. That perhaps explains the switch to comedy in *Mississippi Rainbow* and a musical, *Swing Mikado*.

Ted Ward's difficulties with *Big White Fog* were certainly a case of *de facto* censorship. In that play, protagonist Victor Mason, discouraged by the lack of opportunities for Negroes in America, becomes a follower of Marcus Garvey, but the economic collapse of 1929 sends him and his family on a rapid downhill slide until they face eviction. At the last moment, Mason's son enlists the aid of a white friend, and gathers a group of sympathetic people who prevent their being thrown out. Unfortunately, the father is fatally shot during the struggle.

To many thirties' audiences and critics, any ending where blacks and whites worked together to overcome oppression automatically signaled Communist propaganda. The censors were even sent to rehearsals, but they were unable to discover anything objectionable. Ward's articulation of his goals in writing the play fell on deaf ears, and today, after forty years, he still feels his play was never judged on its merits. His feelings are supported by Langston Hughes, who called it "the greatest, most encompassing play on Negro life that has ever been written" and said, "If it isn't liked by people it is because they are not ready for it, not because it isn't a great play." In spite of its initial box office success, after only ten weeks *Big White Fog* was moved to a local high school where it closed almost immediately for lack of audiences.

Surely one of the most remarkable units was the Seattle Negro Repertory Company, where Burton and Florence James produced *Stevedore, Lysistrata, It Can't Happen Here,* and Ted Browne's folk-opera version of the John Henry legend, *Natural Man.* Browne himself was an invaluable member of the company. He not only wrote and adapted plays, but also helped with casting, coached the actors, and played leading roles.

After a faltering start, the Los Angeles Negro unit produced a wide range of plays, including *Black Empire, Noah, John Henry* by Frank B. Wells, *Androcles and the Lion,* and their own African version of *Macbeth,* directed by Max Pollock. The unit's biggest success was *Run, Little Chillun,* directed by guest director Clarence Muse, which ran for over a year, and then spun off a company that was sent to San Francisco in 1939 to perform at the World's Fair.

Other units too enjoyed their triumphs. The Hartford, Connecticut, group, under the direction of Michael Adrian, was extremely innovative in its choice of productions. Opening with Andreev's *The Sabine Women,* they produced Maurice Maeterlinck's *Death of Tintagiles, The World We Live In* by Josef and Karel Capek, and *It Can't Happen Here.* The production of the Capek play, an "insect comedy" that satirized human society, was enhanced by the choreography and percussion of Alwin Nikolais who volunteered his services for this production. It was Nikolais' first professional credit, and the strange, sudden shifts of movement and tone were an indication of the experimentation that has been a hallmark of his subsequent, distinguished career.

For his leads, Adrian, formerly a technical expert and designer in New York and Hollywood, relied on members of the local Gilpin Players. For fifteen years the group had been a significant part of Hartford cultural life, producing plays by Ridgely Torrence, Paul Green, Eugene O'Neill, and William Shakespeare.

The Hartford unit also staged the works of a young playwright of their own. Ward Courtney had written a powerful living newspaper, *Stars and Bars,* which focused on the state of Connecticut and specifically, his home city of Hartford. With the cooperation and assistance of the Negro unit, the playwright amassed the information necessary to support his view that black people had been repeatedly mistreated in the past, and that abuses still existed in the areas of housing, medical treatment, employment, and the use of public facilities. Another of Courtney's plays, *Trilogy in Black,* used themes from Aeschylus and Euripides to explore the experiences of Negroes after World War I.

A local Newark playwright, Hughes Allison, emerged with *The Trial of Dr. Beck.* The drama of the play revolves around a murder trial, but more important than the guilt or innocence of Dr. Beck in the death of his wife is the focus on con-

Joe Staton in *Natural Man.* Seattle.

Costume designs for *The World We Live In.* Hartford.

Outdoor rehearsal for *Trilogy in Black*. Hartford.

temporary problems of Negro life in America and the straightforward treatment of color prejudice within the race itself. Since *Beck* required a mixed cast, New Jersey WPA officials were apprehensive about its reception, but the production proved to be New Jersey's first popular success, and the first to win unanimous praise from the press. Hallie Flanagan recalls in her book *Arena* that J.J. Shubert said it was the best play he had seen anywhere in the Federal Theatre, and partly at his suggestion, the play was moved to New York where it ran for four weeks.

Subsequently, Allison's extended research as a member of the National Service Bureau resulted in a plan for an ambitious trilogy. Starting with an African prince sold into slavery, Allison would have followed the progress of the young prince, his son, and grandson, up through the Civil War and Reconstruction periods. When the Federal Theatre closed, the first play, *Panyared,* was complete, but there had been no time to plan and execute a production.

In Philadelphia, an inactive Negro unit enjoyed its first successful production with *Prelude to Swing* early in June 1939. The text was written by Carlton Moss, who had been borrowed from the New York Project, and the choreography and direction were by Malvena Fried. The show traced the history of music from Africa to the United States, using a Negro choral group and a swing orchestra. Strong, vigorous, and authentic, *Prelude to Swing* was enjoying excellent press and enthusiastic audiences when Congress shut the Project down on June 30.

CHILDREN WERE an untapped theatrical audience in the 1930s, and the FTP showed great foresight in trying to cultivate them. Outside New York and Los Angeles, productions for children had been few and far between, and even in those cities, few plays were performed by adults. Commercial producers were not interested because box office receipts were not large enough. The Junior League had organized tours of *The Blue Bird* in 1929 and *Treasure Island* in 1931 that had been well attended and well received, but that hardly constituted a children's theatre movement. In contrast, Russia in 1936 had more than 100 theatres, 48 cinemas, and 75 radio stations exclusively producing children's programs.

From the beginning, however, the Federal Theatre realized the importance of children's theatre. Children's plays were educational as well as entertaining, and these children would be the paying audiences of the future. Thus, every major city boasted an FTP unit that produced plays especially for youngsters. Fresh, good scripts were hard to find; so many of the units were at first limited to holiday specials and Saturday morning shows performed by retrained vaudevillians. The large cities, however, soon assigned staff to develop scripts from popular folk and fairy tales like *Cinderella, Aladdin, Hansel and Gretel,*

Alice in Wonderland, Peter Pan, and *Robin Hood,* or from children's classics like *Treasure Island, Little Women,* and *A Christmas Carol.*

In Los Angeles, where 125 people were assigned to the children's theatre, Yasha Frank wrote, designed, and directed original productions of *Hansel and Gretel, Pinocchio,* and *Aladdin. Pinocchio* was such a success that Frank brought it to New York where it played until the FTP closed. While it was still in Los Angeles, Walt Disney attended eight performances; the play made such an impression that he chose *Pinocchio* for his next animated film.

Each of Yasha Frank's shows was a spectacular extravaganza, crammed with color, costume and scene changes, special effects, and music. In *Aladdin,* the dance unit led by Myra Kinch counterpointed the actors' broad opera bouffe manner with four modern dance numbers. Though the critics thought the show had too much action—it was "chaotic" or "diffuse"—the children's comments suggested that the more action, color, and noise, the better. Thirteen thousand children, many of them underprivileged, saw the show during its two-month run in spring 1938. Like all of the children's shows in the Los Angeles FTP, *Aladdin* had to be approved by a committee of educators, police, welfare groups, and service clubs before it opened to the children.

The New York children's unit also had a committee of five well-known educators, who recommended which plays should be produced, as well as trained psychologists who tested and interviewed children in the schools about what they learned from the theatre. New York did not have a dominating creative figure, like Yasha Frank; instead it had a group of young, energetic actors and directors who wanted to do children's shows that had a definite moral. *Revolt of the Beavers,* of course, was their clearest (and most controversial) attempt to educate as well as entertain, but in their popular productions of *The Emperor's New Clothes* and *Flight,* a new play about the history of aviation by Oscar Saul and Lou Lantz, the same motive is apparent.

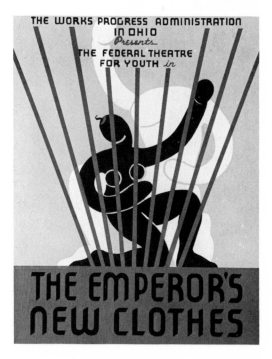

The Emperor's New Clothes, by Charlotte Chorpenning, dramatizes the foolish vanity of authorities, the power of conformity, and the force of common sense—even if it comes from a child. Maurice Clark directed the New York production and Lehman Engel composed the music. Sam Bonnell, a Broadway veteran of *Street Scene* and *Counsellor-at-Law,* played the wily Zan, and his partner, Zar, was played by the young Jules Dassin. Together they were especially adept at involving young audiences and adlibbing when the youngsters joined in the action. Over a quarter of a million people saw the show during its one-and-a-half-year run, many of them children in schools, hospitals, and orphanages. Following New York's lead, seven other cities produced *The Emperor's New Clothes* as well. This was augmented by hundreds of schoolroom adaptations, since the New York unit, like many of the others,

Federal Theatre gave me a chance to show that marionettes can be very high-class adult entertainment. We could go into the classics, which is something others hadn't done; they were still doing the fairy tales for children. . . . The variety shows I did were adult productions. The Federal Theatre was sponsoring a whole new program in theatre, and marionettes had to get out of the rut.

RALPH CHESSE,
head of the California marionette unit

String Fever. New York City.

provided instructions and material for teachers. The large cast usually gave every child in the class a chance to perform.

The children's unit in Gary, Indiana, was an FTP exception in that children were the performers. During the two-year life of this unit, children ranging in age from four to eighteen years gave nearly 180 performances—many of them celebrating ethnic holidays with folk dramas and native costumes—before a total of sixty-seven thousand children. The actors performed in schools, parks and the children's community center, which had formerly been the offices of the Aetna Powder and Explosives Company. The buildings were converted into a theatre, rehearsal hall, and workshop space, in which the children were introduced to the various behind-the-scenes skills that make a theatre.

The desire to reveal the craft as well as the art of theatre was also a hallmark of many of the twenty-two marionette units scattered across the country. The puppeteers would encourage the children to watch the backstage action and frequently offered classes in the building and handling of puppets. Involving people in the making of the marionettes was also an effective way of supplementing the small staff assigned to these units, most of which were poor cousins to the "legitimate" theatre. Despite the low budgets, the Federal Theatre treated marionettes as an integral and valuable part of a people's theatre movement. The FTP employed more puppeteers in New York City alone than had previously worked throughout the country.

Children's classics and variety shows were the staples of most of these units. Remo Bufano in New York City designed and directed *Treasure Island, Oliver Twist,* and *Sherlock Holmes.* In Los Angeles, a puppet van directed by Bob Bromley toured the parks with a variety show based on *Don Quixote.* With its magic tricks, *Aladdin* was a favorite of many of the units. However, even marionette shows for children provided an occasion for a local skirmish in the running battle between official support of theatre in general, and censorship of particular plays. When the Los Angeles School Board found Hans Christian Anderson's *Tinderbox* objectionable because of its "political significance," the play was never performed.

The marionette units, which presented an average of 100 shows a week, were not limited to children's plays. Puppets built by Bil Baird were used to portray the Seven Deadly Sins in Orson Welles' *Doctor Faustus.* On the West Coast, Ralph Chessé, following the lead of Blanding Sloan, adapted James Stephens *Crock of Gold* and Eugene O'Neill's *Emperor Jones* for puppets. These shows were presented in the same theatres as the regular FTP productions, and Chessé had to develop new methods in lighting and sound in order to diminish the stage space. The Buffalo Historical Marionettes presented plays on safety and history. The plays, including such diverse fare as *The Constitution, Eli Whitney and the Cotton Gin,* and *Niagara Frontier,* were intended primarily for an adult audience. *Death Takes the Wheel,* which dramatized the danger of careless driving, was sponsored by various civic groups as it toured throughout the region as far south as West Virginia.

The circus was another form of entertainment sponsored by the FTP that appealed to both children and adults. Jugglers, cyclists, aerialists, tightrope walkers, strong men and women, clowns, hoofers, and tappers entertained children of all ages. There were few wild animals since, as Hallie Flanagan explained, "There were no elephants on relief." Fortunately, they were given one, though he was a challenge to government red tape. Japino was also a challenge to keep penned; the newspapers reported his escape in Ridgewood one week, and in Forest Hills the next.

The largest circus—250 performers in sixty acts—was, of course, located in the New York area, but a number of them also toured regionally. Many of the performers belonged to families who had been in the circus for years. Like vaudevillians, their talents were less in demand as the great train tours became a victim of the Depression. Younger performers were not attracted to the circus as they once were, though there were notable exceptions like Burt Lancaster, who began his career as an aerialist.

Though the heyday of the circus might have passed, the greatest shows on earth could still draw massive crowds. Half-a-million people saw the New York circus during its first six-month tour. One of these performances was a benefit for children in settlement houses scattered throughout the city. The WPA transported, fed, and entertained—without an accident—the more than eight thousand disadvantaged children attending the shows. For many, the circus bordered on the periphery of the theatre world, but it offered a viable alternative for those whose talents were not as saleable on the "legitimate" stage. In a changing economic order, the circus was a good final example of the Federal Theatre's importance in the lives of those who needed a little respite.

THE POLITICS

ONLY IN THE RECENT past has American drama followed the long heritage of drama in other places and times and become conspicuously political. The Federal Theatre was central to the development of an energetic, socially conscious theatre in America. As Hallie Flanagan wrote, in a 1936 *New Republic* essay, "Drama, through rhythmic speech, dynamic movement and contagious listening, can influence human thought and lead to human action." This idea that drama can affect society was especially appealing and

Burt Lancaster and Nick Cravat. Circus, New York City.

powerful in the thirties. It was a decade when new theatre groups like the Theatre Union were formed to "produce plays that deal boldly with the deep-going social conflicts, the economic, emotional, and cultural problems that confront the majority of the people," and when successful, traditional playwrights wrote plays of social protest, like Maxwell Anderson's *Both Your Houses* (1933), and Robert Sherwood's *Idiot's Delight* (1936).

During the thirties, labor theatre groups were so popular they were able to organize a national conference in 1932 and create an association, The League of Workers' Theatres. Amateur groups acting in lofts and little theatres expanded agit-prop (agitation-propaganda) into such popular successes as *Waiting For Lefty* (1935) by Clifford Odets and *Bury the Dead* (1936) by Irwin Shaw. Theatre, it was declared, was a weapon.

How effective a weapon is always open to debate. One can argue that the thirties were not the "Red Decade," and that only about 10 percent of the plays produced were concerned with social or political topics. Yet one has to recognize that the apparent failure of capitalism engendered a radical examination of American beliefs and institutions in a significant number of plays. These plays and the various groups and collectives that performed them, attempted to show how capitalism tolerated or encouraged racism, war, poverty, and other social ills. They attracted new working-class audiences to the theatre, where they could see powerful commentaries on their society. The bewildered middle class were also in search of insight into their lives and culture, which drama could provide.

It is within this theatrical tradition that the FTP inevitably, but deliberately, placed itself. Hallie Flanagan tried to enunciate its mission in frequent speeches and essays. In the essay "Democracy and the Drama," she wrote: "The Federal Theatre is a pioneer theatre because it is part of a tremendous re-thinking, re-building and re-dreaming of America. . . . These activities represent the new frontier in America, a frontier against disease, dirt, poverty, illiteracy, unemployment and despair, and at the same time against selfishness, special privilege and social apathy. And in the struggle for a better life, our actors know what they are talking about; the Federal Theatre, being their theatre, becomes not merely a decoration but a vital force in our democracy."

Despite all of the fine talk about a national theatre that would produce new plays on serious subjects, the FTP had to confront the reality of government control and federal funding through the WPA. When Elmer Rice accepted the job as head of the New York City Federal Theatre, he expressed his doubts about whether Harry Hopkins could keep his promise that the FTP would be "free, adult, uncensored." Rice's first big production, *Ethiopia*, settled the matter in his mind. The play was a factual dramatization of the Italian takeover of Ethiopia and the responses of the Western democracies. When the New York unit tried to get a recording of Roosevelt's radio broadcast about the Ethiopian war, they were questioned about the need for the recording, and then ordered not to impersonate any foreign dignitaries in Federal Theatre plays. For Rice this was a clear sign of the censorship the government would continually exercise over the FTP. The subsequent arguments and eventual compromise—quotations of foreign officials could be used, but no impersonations—failed to convince him otherwise. He threatened to resign unless the order was rescinded. Jacob Baker, the head of the white-collar division of the WPA, responded with a letter that read, in part:

> *When difficulties have arisen in the past in connection with the operation of the Federal Theatre Project within the framework of the governmental structure, you have proposed either to resign or to take the difficulties to the press. Now that a problem has arisen in connection with a dramatization that may affect our international relations, you renew your proposal of resignation in a telegram to Mr. Hopkins. This time I accept it . . .*

Rice held a news conference and a dress rehearsal of the play for the press, which responded with headlines and impassioned articles defending Ethiopia. The tremendous press reaction and Rice's resignation may actually have had the effect of forestalling other acts of censorship from Washington. The WPA, especially the Arts Projects, was controversial enough that federal administrators generally tried to avoid publicity. While most people recognized the need for some form of relief, many were skeptical of the "work" done in the Arts Projects. Hopkins and his aides spent a disproportionate amount of time responding to charges of boondoggling on the Arts Projects; they did not want to face criticism about government propaganda and censorship.

Nevertheless, another instance of federal censorship occurred sixteen months later. John Houseman and Orson Welles, after establishing impressive reputations through such FTP hits as the "voodoo" *Macbeth* and *Doctor Faustus,* had chosen to produce Marc Blitzstein's folk opera, *The Cradle Will Rock.* The play, a prounion account of a steel strike with most of its action cast in a court room, was scheduled to open on June 16, 1937. On June 12, Hallie Flanagan received a memorandum that "no openings of new productions shall take place until after the beginning of the coming fiscal year." The stated reason was the need for reorganization after the expected cuts in appropriations, but most people viewed it as WPA censorship. No other new production, musical performance, or art show was scheduled to open during the last two weeks of June.

Apparently, officials in Washington thought the play too "dangerous" for the times. Industrial cities in the midwest were racked with labor strife as the CIO tried to organize "little steel." While *Cradle Will Rock* was in rehearsal, workers, goons, and police were battling in such places as Chicago (ten died in

Rehearsal for *The Cradle Will Rock*. New York City.

the Memorial Day riot), Lansing, Youngstown, Monroe, Kansas City, and Johnstown, as well as in numerous mining towns. Washington officials were trying to check the violence without overtly choosing sides. At the same time, the WPA was scheduled to appear before congressional appropriation committees. Cuts of 25-30 percent were expected in the white-collar division, and many feared the Arts Projects would be cut entirely. WPA officials were anxious not to offend Congress, and wanted the potentially controversial *Cradle Will Rock* to open (if at all), after Congress had decided on a budget. John Houseman recalled the explosiveness of the situation in his autobiography, *Run-Through*: "What Hallie had taken, in mid-February, for a dynamic piece of Americana had turned by early June (with the WPA in turmoil and steel strikes on the front page) into a time bomb that threatened to bring the entire project tumbling about her head."

Houseman's autobiography describes in colorful detail his unit's response. Despite enormous, unsolved problems, they insisted that the show would go on outside of the WPA, for artistic, if not political, reasons. They had to find a theatre that was vacant but ready, replace the orchestra because of musician's union demands, satisfy Equity's ruling that their members should not act in a play that still belonged to the WPA, and then let their audience know about the decisions. On opening night the audience marched twenty blocks to the Venice Theatre where Marc Blitzstein played a rented upright piano alone on stage. Members of the cast, which included Will Geer, Howard da Silva, and Hiram Sherman, rose to speak or sing their parts from their seats, thereby satisfying Equity's ruling.

By all accounts the performance was one of the great moments in American theatre history. But Welles and Houseman were now no longer part of the WPA (*Cradle* was the birth of the Mercury Theatre), and the Federal Theatre had one more mark against its record in Washington.

These celebrated instances of censorship by federal officials were rare, given the number of shows produced by the FTP and the traditional hostility toward theatre shared by many groups. Local harassment and censorship, on the other hand, was a frequent and continual problem for the Federal Theatre. The state WPA administrators, who controlled the local FTP unit's budget, were generally political appointees and not always sympathetic to theatre.

The most glaring example was Lieutenant Colonel Donald Connolly of California. He insisted upon approving everything, from materials (even five kilowatt bulbs), to play selection. He canceled scheduled productions of Paul Peters' and George Sklar's *Stevedore*, a play about race and union conflicts, and Elmer Rice's *Judgment Day*, a play about fascism. He fired Gilmor Brown (who had come from the Pasadena Playhouse at the inception of the Project), then forced the resignation of his successor, George Gerwing, and his successor,

James R. Ullmann. Protests about the Colonel's actions were sent to Hopkins from Burgess Meredith and Henry Fonda on behalf of Actor's Equity and the National Council of Freedom; the Screen Writer's Guild, the ACLU, and the Arts Union Conference joined in the protest. *Judgment Day* was reinstated, but Colonel Connolly continued his autocratic ways until he voluntarily left the WPA in the spring of 1939.

Similar tampering by the state WPA administrator occurred in other places, though it was not as thorough. In Louisiana and Missouri, the state administrators would not let their theatre units participate in the nationwide, simultaneous productions of *It Can't Happen Here*. In Washington state, after the opening night performance of an adaptation of Aristophanes' *Lysistrata*, performed by the Seattle Negro unit, the WPA head canceled the play because his wife thought it obscene. The Illinois state director also closed down another reportedly "obscene" play, Paul Green's *Hymn to the Rising Sun*, a drama about prison chain gangs. The play was to be performed by the Negro unit, but on opening night with over 300 patrons standing in front of the theatre, it was announced that the production would be delayed a few days "for purely technical reasons." It never opened and the director, Charles DeSheim, resigned in protest. Supposedly the show would "alienate people from the legitimate theatre because of its portrayal of nauseating brutality." Ironically, *Hymn to the Rising Sun* had won a Chicago play contest when it was produced commercially ten months earlier.

The Chicago FTP also had to face the whims of Mayor Ed Kelly, who had a long-standing reputation for prohibiting plays for the good of his citizens. He had stopped productions of *Tobacco Road, The Children's Hour,* and other lesser-known plays before the FTP was established, so it came as no surprise when he forbade a production of *Model Tenements* by Meyer Levin early in 1936. The play, about a grocer who overextends himself by building tenements and the subsequent effect he has on the families who inhabit his housing project, suggests that better tenements are not a solution; instead, sweeping changes are needed in the social and economic system. According to Levin in his autobiography, *In Search*, it was not his radical views that were objectionable. A local priest acted as the mayor's unofficial censor, and after Levin made the priest's suggested changes (striking out a few damns and hells and putting an undershirt on a shirtless man), the play was approved. But the damage was done: the FTP supervisor had changed, a new schedule had been set, and *Model Tenements* abandoned.

Not all of the Federal Theatre's political problems came from officials outside the Project; many of them originated among the Project's personnel. Again, one must remember the times. Papers carried daily items about the Spanish Civil War, the rise of the Third Reich, Japanese aggression in China, and the im-

Lysistrata. Seattle.

pressive economic growth of the Soviet Union. At home, labor troubles, unemployment, racial violence, and, of course, the Roosevelt programs, dominated the news. The Great Depression forced many people to question economic, social, and political systems, and men with a vision of the future—whether they were Father Coughlin or Father Divine, Earl Browder or Franklin Roosevelt—were popular and persuasive. One seemed continually to face the common refrain, "Which side are you on?"

Though it was illegal to engage in any political activity on Project time or facilities, separating out politics was hard for many to do. With a number of people always waiting to be assigned to a play, and with union rules restricting performers to only four hours of rehearsal a day, there was plenty of free time for nontheatrical business. In New York, decisions about which theatre unit or which union to join, were frequently considered political. The experimental unit, which produced Em Jo Basshe's *Snickering Horses* (antiwar) and Michael Gold and Michael Blankfort's *Battle Hymn* (a defense of John Brown), was abolished during staff cuts partly because of the alleged intensity of the political activity in the unit. Rumors around the children's unit, which gathered attention for its production of *Revolt of the Beavers*, claimed that Communist and anti-Communist blacklists were used to make personnel and staff decisions. Whenever personnel reductions were ordered, charges and rumors immediately flourished—this supervisor was a Communist, that one a racist, another anti-union. When Zvee Scooler was ordered to cut his Anglo-Yiddish unit by half its size he refused, both because he felt his supervisors were discriminating and because he did not want to be open to similar charges himself. Scooler was fired and his unit disbanded.

The Federal Theatre was not a closed shop, but unions could present grievances, so considerable pressure was placed on unaffiliated workers. According to Hallie Flanagan, union affiliation made up the "greatest single administrative problem in New York City" (elsewhere the problem was not as great). Research, administrative, and maintenance workers, as well as dancers and many Jewish and Negro actors, did not belong to unions. In New York most of them joined the City Projects Council, the WPA white-collar affiliate of the Workers' Alliance, a union of unemployed relief clients. The Communist-led Workers' Alliance was much more strident and forceful in its demands than the older stage unions. It led strikes, protest marches, picket lines, and letter campaigns. When the first large-scale cuts in WPA personnel were announced in the spring of 1936, it organized a one-day work stoppage—seven thousand of the nine thousand WPA workers in New York City stayed home on May 27. Because it represented WPA workers in many different kinds of projects, it also received more attention in Washington. Congressmen charged that through the Workers' Alliance, Communists controlled the Arts Projects. The administration, fearing more public attention, tried to appease the union, which was often informed of departmental decisions before the project administrators. Since many of the people who belonged to the Workers' Alliance were not performers (the actors, stagehands, writers, and others closely connected to the stage had their own unions), ill feelings and bad press arose when cuts were ordered. Some performers and outside observers could not appreciate the need for administrative and maintenance help in a large government project, and charged that the Workers' Alliance dictated who was to be fired. Protests and meetings would follow each reduction or reorganization. The Federal Theatre actually had less trouble with the Workers' Alliance and other unions than most of the WPA projects, primarily because the FTP administrators were clearly prounion. Hallie Flanagan and her assistants spent countless hours working out grievances with union representatives. They continually urged the union leaders not to wreck the whole Project with their infighting and occasionally impossible demands.

"Lookit, I'm paying 55¢ for standing room and a week ago I could have seen the same dancers on the picket line for nothing."

WHEN THE HOUSE Un-American Activities Committee (HUAC) first convened in August 1938 to investigate charges of "un-American propaganda activities" in this country, the Federal Theatre Project was an irresistible target. A vocal minority of FTP personnel had created the image of a Communist-controlled project racked by controversy and committed to something more than just relief; HUAC members were also quick to learn that attacks on theatre made good press; it appealed to a longstanding bias against theatre and to growing popular and congressional disenchantment with the massive New Deal relief programs.

Congressman J. Parnell Thomas, a Republican committee member from New Jersey (who was jailed years later for defrauding the government), set the sensationalist tone of the FTP investigation at a press conference, weeks before the committee convened, when he announced, "It is apparent from the startling evidence received thus far that the Federal Theatre Project not only is serving as a branch of the Communistic organization but is also one more link in the vast and unparalleled New Deal propaganda machine . . . I shall strongly urge that our committee dig deeply into the entire Federal Theatre Project, which seemingly is infested with radicals from top to bottom." He cited as examples of plays with "Communistic leanings," *Prologue to Glory* (about young Lincoln), *Haiti*, and *One-Third of a Nation*. HUAC Chairman Martin Dies, a Texas Democrat, promised that investigations would be thorough, with "no shooting in the dark." But the transcript of the FTP hearings is a sad and embarrassing account of what one historian has called "one of the weirdest collections of evidence ever permitted before the committee."

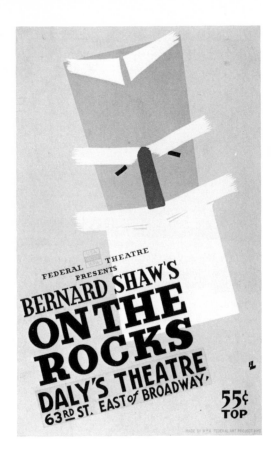

The primary source of the evidence and the committee's first witness was Hazel Huffman, a former WPA mail clerk, who claimed she had been ordered by a WPA administrator to "analyze" FTP mail. Her rambling and occasionally pointless testimony was filled with hearsay evidence, conjecture, inconsistency, half-truths, and untruths. She charged that Hallie Flanagan's "active participation and interest in things Communist" was apparent in her 1926 trip to Russia, her review of workers' theatres in *Theatre Arts Monthly* in 1931, and her play *Can You Hear Their Voices?* adding that Flanagan's "Communistic sympathies, tendencies and methods of organization are being used in the Federal Theatre Project . . . to the detriment of the workers and in violation of the act of Congress." According to Huffman, Communist plays were "the rule" at the FTP; her examples included the living newspapers, Shaw's *On The Rocks*, Lewis' *It Can't Happen Here*, Green's *Hymn to the Rising Sun*, Sklar and Maltz's *Revolt of the Beavers*, and Blitzstein's *Cradle Will Rock*—twenty-eight plays in all. She was followed by nine lesser witnesses, most of whom, like Huffman, had been fired or refused promotions because of lack of ability.

Each witness either volunteered or was prompted to talk about matters beyond their knowledge or experience. For instance, Henry Frank, of the New York payroll department, described the living newspaper bureau in the following exchange with Representative Harold Mosier, (D-Ohio):

MOSIER: *Tell the Committee, if you know, whether or not they are propaganda plays . . . for the Communist Party or the Soviet Government.*

FRANK: *That is the only thing they look for . . . they do not try to put on a drama; they do not try to put on a comic (sic); they do not try to put on a classic; they simply look for plays that are propaganda, and that is why they have had such a large force of research workers . . . about fifty . . . who do nothing but trace records and news items on anything that relates to propaganda.*

The transcript also reveals the basic misunderstanding by the committee of the purpose and operations of the FTP. One committee member asked Huffman, "Who is writing these plays—relief workers or people on the project?" FTP officials felt sure that a thorough, detailed written response would dispel the rumors and innuendos that marked the committee hearings. Hallie Flanagan repeatedly wrote Chairman Dies asking for the opportunity to testify. Her staff prepared a two-hundred page brief that answered every charge, listed groups that booked theatre parties, and included sample play reviews, staff resumes, and office memos. WPA officials, on the other hand, ignored the initial testimony and press headlines. They felt a battle for headlines would be demeaning and useless. Only after the committee turned its attention to the Federal Writers' Project did they call for a chance to respond to the charges.

Throughout the fall, Flanagan and her assistants waited their turn. The committee seemed uninterested in their views and continued to release statements to the press that made it clear the committee had already made up its mind. Chairman Dies told reporters in mid-October that the Theatre and Writers' Projects were "doing more to spread Communist propaganda than the Communist party itself." By the time Hallie Flanagan was called to testify on December 6, 1938, she not only had to correct huge chunks of erroneous testimony, but she also had to speak before a committee that had continually made public statements against the FTP. Throughout the morning she defended her past actions and present views, and the Project's play selections, while trying to educate the committee about the nature and role of theatre. The following is a typical exchange between the witnesses and the chairman:

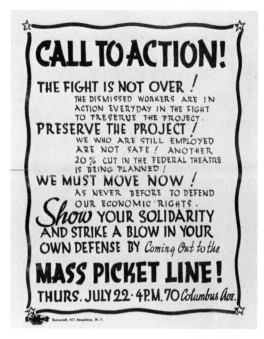

CHM. DIES: *Do you not also think that since the Federal Theatre Project is an agency of the Government and that all of our people support it through their tax money, . . . that no play should ever be produced which undertakes to portray the interests of one class to the disadvantage of another class, even though that might be accurate, even though factually there may be justification normally for that, yet because of the very fact that we are using taxpayers' money to produce plays, do you not think it is questionable . . . ?*

MRS. FLANAGAN: *I think we strive for objectivity, but I think the whole history of plays in the theatre would indicate that any dramatist holds a passionate brief for the things he is saying . . . practically any play from the beginning of time has been loaded with some dramatist's ideas and emotions.*

Through it all she remained remarkably composed and restrained. She realized the ultimate seriousness of the moment even during the investigation's most comic moment:

MRS. FLANAGAN: *. . . this ambition alone invests their [workers' theaters] undertaking with a certain Marlowesque madness.*

MR. STARNES: *You are quoting from this Marlowe. Is he a Communist?*

MRS. FLANAGAN: *I am very sorry. I was quoting from Christopher Marlowe.*

MR. STARNES: *Tell us who Marlowe is, so we can get the proper reference, because that is all we want to do.*

MRS. FLANAGAN: *Put in the record that he was the greatest dramatist in the period of Shakespeare, immediately preceding Shakespeare.*

In *Arena*, her history of the FTP, Hallie Flanagan recalled, "the room rocked

GIVE A DAY'S PAY TO SAVE W.P.A.

CITY PROJECTS COUNCIL

DON'T TREAD ON ME

with laughter, but I did not laugh. Eight thousand people might lose their jobs because a Congressional Committee had so pre-judged us that even the classics were Communistic!" When lunchtime arrived, Hallie Flanagan was dismissed. The committee did not want to confront this witness any longer, nor did they enter the FTP brief into the record.

A month later HUAC issued its report with only a single paragraph devoted to the Federal Theatre: "A rather large number of employees . . . of the Project are either members of the Communist party or sympathizers with the Communist party. It is also clear that certain employees felt under the compulsion to join the Worker's Alliance in order to retain their jobs." The report was anticlimactic. The statement was significantly more restrained than everyone expected, but the damage the Dies' committee had done to the FTP was so extensive that it would never recover. Regardless of what the final report actually said, the months of unanswered charges and sensational headlines had firmly equated the Project with Communist subversion.

When the new WPA budget was sent to the House in the spring of 1939, the Congress was in no mood to appropriate huge sums of money for relief without changes in the agencies. The Federal Theatre was a natural scapegoat, and WPA officials tacitly agreed not to put up a fight to save it. After all, it was less than one-half percent of the 875 million dollars requested by Roosevelt.

Besides the old claims of boondoggling and Communist control, the FTP had to overcome a new charge that touched the heart of an FTP paradox: was the Federal Theatre a relief agency or a national theatre? According to the chairman of the House Committee on Appropriations, Clifton Woodrum, the Project had forgotten its purpose—"to furnish relief assistance to unemployed theatrical people"—in its desire to "enter the field of amusement and entertainment," in competition with private enterprise. Hallie Flanagan was convinced that the record of the past three years proved they could meet both objectives. But with the beginning of a wartime economy, the House clearly thought it was time to cut back on relief, and it was unwilling to support a national theatre.

The FTP staff organized a belated campaign to save the Project, enlisting the aid of prominent theatre and film personalities, theatre critics, and union leaders. Their help and the last-minute efforts to save the Federal Theatre are finely detailed in Jane Mathews' *The Federal Theatre Project, 1935-1939.* Their efforts were more effective in the Senate than in the House, where the FTP simply could not appeal to many congressmen's interests—the retrenchment of the past year had forced many of the smaller units in the South and West to close. The Senate Relief Bill included funding for the Federal Theatre, but the House version did not. In conference the FTP was cut as part of a compromise package. Roosevelt had little choice; a veto would have ended the whole relief program on the next day. While signing the bill, Roosevelt remarked, "This singles out a special group of professional people for a denial of work in their profession. It is discrimination of the worst type."

The Project was over. They had one month to close down and pack up what had taken almost four years to build. At its best, the Federal Theatre Project had fulfilled Hallie Flanagan's vision of what theatre, especially a national theatre, must accomplish:

> *We live in a changing world: man is whispering through space, soaring to the stars in ships, flinging miles of steel and glass into the air. Shall the theatre continue to huddle in the confines of a painted box set? The movies, in their kaleidoscopic speed and juxtaposition of external objects and internal emotions are seeking to find visible and audible expression for the tempo and the psychology of our time. The stage too must experiment—with ideas, with psychological relationships of men and women, with speech and rhythm forms, with dance and movement, with color and light—or it must and should become a museum product.*

> *In an age of terrific implications as to wealth and poverty, as to the function of government, as to peace and war, as to the relation of the artist to all these forces, the theatre must grow up. The theatre must become conscious of the implications of the changing social order, or the changing social order will ignore, and rightly, the implications of the theatre.*

THE FEDERAL THEATRE

HALLIE FLANAGAN
National Director

PHILIP W. BARBER
Director for N.Y.C.

PROJECT 891

presents

"HORSE EATS HAT"

BY
EDWIN DENBY and **ORSON WELLES**
based on a play by Labiche
Costumes and Settings by Nat Karson
Directed by Orson Welles

Music by Paul Bowles—Orchestrated by Virgil Thomson
Lighting by Feder

The Federal Theatre Project is part of the W.P.A. program. However, the viewpoint expressed in the plays is not necessarily that of the W.P.A. or any other agency of the Government.

CAST OF CHARACTERS

Freddy ....Joseph Cotten
Mugglethorpe ....Orson Welles
Entwhistle ....George Duthie
Uncle Adolphe.......................................Donald MacMillian
Queeper ....Dana Stevens
Bobbin...Hiram Sherman
Grimshot, Lieut. of Cavalry.............................Sidney Smith
Joseph ....Harry McKee
Gustave, Viscount....................................France Bendtsen
Augustus ....Edgerton Paul
Myrtle Mugglethorp...................................Virginia Welles
Agatha Entwhistle....................................Paula Laurence
Tillie ....Arlene Francis
The Countess..Sarah Burton
Daisy ....Henriette Kaye
Clotilda ....Lucy Rodriquez
Corporal ....Bernard Savage
Butler ....Walter Burton
First Footman...Steven Carter
Second Footman..J. Headley
Raguso ....Enrico Cellini
Berkowitz, a friend of Queeper's, in jail................George Barter

WEDDING GUESTS—Ellen Worth, Arabella St. James, Marie Jones, Hattie Rappaport, Anna Gold, Myron Paulson, Wallace Acton, Pell Dentler, George Leach and Bill Baird.

TILLIE'S GIRLS—Peggy Hartley, Terry Carlson, Lee Molnar, Gloria Sheldon, Teresa Alvarez, Opal Essant, June Thorne, Mildred Colt and Geraldine Law.

COUNTESS' GUESTS—Georgia Empry, Solomon Goldstein, May Angela, Lawrence Hawley, Margaret Maley, Jack Smith, Mary Kukavski, Elizabeth Malone, Ann Morton, Helena Rapport, Helene Korsun, Nina Salama, Julia Fassett, Jane Hale, Jane Johnson, Michael Callaghan, Don Harward, Walter LeRoy, Harry Merchant and Warren Goddard.

CITIZENS NIGHT PATROL—Arthur Wood, James Perry, Victor Wright, Robert Hopkins, Craig Gordon, Harry Singer, Frank Kelly, Bernard Lewis, Henry Russelle, Charles Uday, George Smithfield, Henry Laird, Edwin Hemmer, George Armstrong, Jerry Hitchcock and Tod Brown.

Horse.......................Carol King and Edwin Denby
At the Nickelodeon...........................Edgerton Paul

PROLOGUE
In the Park

ACT I
At Freddie's

ACT II
Tillie's Hat Store

ACT III
At the Countess'

INTERMISSION 15 MINUTES

ACT IV
At the Entwhistle's

ACT V
Bandolia Square

The Place: Paris   The Time: 1908

———o———

Managing Producer...John Houseman
Assistant Producer...Ted Thomas
Musical Director...Virgil Thomson
General Stage Manager...................................Thomas Carnahan
Stage Manager..W. Greenbaum
Assistant Stage Manager.......................................Carol King
House Manager..Al Herman
Dept. of Information....................................701 Eighth Avenue

MEdallion 3-5962—Ex. 74

ORCHESTRA
By courtesy of the Federal Music Project of New York City
Conductor..Jacques Gottlieb

Pianos—Herman Magaliff, George Couvreur
Military ensemble under the direction of Edna White, Trumpeteer.
Settings executed by Federal Theatre Workshop.
Horse executed by Bill Baird.

MAXINE ELLIOTT'S THEATRE
109 West 39th Street   CHickering 4-5715

HORSE EATS HAT

WPA Federal Theatre
Project 891 · presents

HORSE EATS HAT

MAXINE
ELLIOTT'S
THEATRE
109 WEST 39th ST.

AFTER A SUCCESSFUL year in the New York Negro theatre unit, John Houseman and Orson Welles moved downtown to the Maxine Elliott Theatre to organize a unit that would perform revivals of classics. They had done their job well in Harlem, giving the Lafayette Theatre group a sense of pride, a clear organization, and a string of successes. Now they wanted to try something different.

Houseman and Welles assembled a varied, talented cast and production crew, bringing with them from the Lafayette unit both Abe Feder for lighting and Virgil Thomson for orchestration. They encouraged new players, like Joseph Cotten and Arlene Francis, to join this WPA unit, soon to be named "Project 891," after its bureaucratic number. With only a few changes, this group formed the Mercury Theatre less than a year later when WPA officials censored their production of Marc Blitzstein's *Cradle Will Rock*. (*See* p. 27.) The Mercury Theatre, for its two brief and famous seasons, upheld the ideal Houseman and Welles aimed for in Project 891—to produce for a popular audience classical plays with a modern flair.

Horse Eats Hat was their improbable first production choice for Project 891, opening September 26, 1936. It was a loose translation of Eugene Labiche's *Un chapeau de paille d'Italie*, a nineteenth-century French farce. L.N., the reviewer for the *New York Times* tried to explain the play: "It has no beginning or end, and lacks rhyme and reason. It tells of a horse that eats a hat, and the owner of the horse must get the owner of the hat another hat because she can't go home to her husband without it. Because—well, Edwin Denby and Orson Welles have adapted the play from a French farce, and French farces are what they are."

The production was noisy, colorful, and frenzied. Welles' legendary energy generally found its outlet in the exuberance of Elizabethan plays, and in his hands *Horse Eats Hat* had an Elizabethan quality with its crowd scenes, quick shifts in tone, and general clamor. The reviews and audience response were "mixed." Part of the audience was unsure whether the Federal Theatre should sponsor this sort of extravaganza. Everett Dirksen, then a young congressman, thought the whole thing was "salacious tripe." Another part of the audience loved it and came frequently—one person reportedly saw the play twenty-one times in succession.

Joseph Cotten and Virginia Welles enjoy one of the few tranquil moments in the frenzied production. This role was Cotten's first Broadway success; he stayed with Orson Welles in the Mercury Theatre and followed him to Hollywood to act in *Citizen Kane*.

His inquisitive horse having interrupted a lover's meeting, Freddie must defend himself against the outraged Husser (Sydney Smith), only to help revive the embarrassed Mrs. Entwhistle (Paula Laurence).

After checking the script with his wife
Virginia, Welles directs the antics of Arlene
Francis and Joseph Cotten.

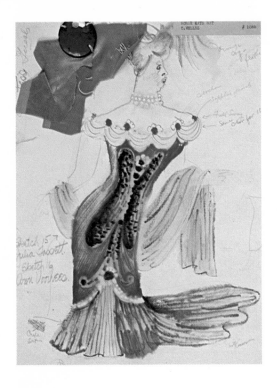

So relentless was our determination to entertain our audience that, even during intermission, we gave them no respite. Before they had a chance to rise from their seats, after the chaotic climax of the first act, their attention was caught by a clear brazen blast from the right mezzanine box, where a lady trumpeter in a white satin hussar's uniform, complete with cape and shako trimmed with gold, rendered a loud and brilliant solo of Paul Bowles' variations on the Carnaval de Venise, with Hiawatha as an encore. Hardly had her well-merited applause begun to diminish when, in the upper stage box opposite, a mechanical piano broke furiously into "Rosy O'Grady." The noise must have disturbed the sleep of a drunken guest, a member of the Countess' ill-fated party, who now appeared, lost and leering, from behind the pianola, seemed to feel himself trapped up there and started to climb out over the edge of the box into the auditorium. Unsteadily, with many slips and falls, he got first one leg and then the other over the side of the box; then, with a great cry, he slipped and fell and remained hanging, head down, with one foot caught in the railing, swinging like an erratic pendulum over the heads of the audience while the mechanical piano switched to Liszt's "Hungarian Rhapsody No. 2." The young acrobat's name was Bil Baird; later in the run, growing careless with success, he slipped, fell and broke his leg in several places.

JOHN HOUSEMAN, *from* Run-Through

John Houseman and Orson Welles swap problems during a rehearsal break. Houseman (whose excellent memoir, *Run-Through*, describes his FTP days), came to the theatre after a successful start in the grain export business. He was chosen to head the Lafayette unit in Harlem with Rose McClendon.

Welles joined the Federal Theatre when Houseman invited him to direct the "voodoo" *Macbeth*. Welles was already a seasoned performer when he began directing for the FTP at the age of twenty-one. He had played Broadway, toured with Katherine Cornell in *Romeo and Juliet*, acted for the Gate Theatre in Dublin, and performed in various popular radio shows, including "The Shadow." Together, Welles and Houseman became the most innovative and effective team in the Federal Theatre.

I remember not only Horse Eats Hat itself, but an odd circumstance surrounding the performance. With a large attending audience one night at the Maxine Elliott Theatre on Thirty-ninth Street, only two individuals audibly enjoyed its performance.

I had gone to see it alone. From the moment the curtain rose I found it hilarious. So did someone else seated some distance from me whom I couldn't see. We were volcanic islets of mirth in a sea of silence. Hearing another man laughing as much as I was kept me from being intimidated by the general apathy.

The last scene of the first act was a ballroom in a Paris mansion. It was crowded with guests waltzing to the music of an improbably large band of zimbalon players, augmenting the conventional orchestra in the pit. The dancers floated around a fountain in the center of the ballroom. (You must remember another object of the Federal Theatre was to provide jobs for technicians.)

The fugitive hero of the piece, played by the young Joseph Cotten, whom we had seen being chased by half the population of Paris, dashed onto the stage pursued by gendarmes. The dancers and the music

stopped as the hero leaped like a gymnast to the branches of a chandelier. As it swung back and forth, pistols were whipped out from full-dress coats and décolleté gowns. Everyone began firing at the young man on the chandelier. Simultaneously, the fountain yet rose higher, drenching the fugitive until the chandelier, on an impulse of its own, rose like a balloon out of range. While the shooting kept up, ten liveried footmen made their way through the crowd. As the curtain began to fall they announced to the audience with unruffled dignity: "Supper is served." The moment the curtain shut off the scene, a lady cornetist in a hussar's uniform appeared in an upper box and offered a virtuoso demonstration of her skill.

As the audience and I moved into the lobby, I spotted a man wiping tears of pleasure from his eyes. It was my friend John Dos Passos. For our own security— in case the second act proved as funny as the first—we sat in adjacent vacant seats we found in a rear row. For the rest of the evening we screamed with laughter together.

MARC CONNELLY, *from* Voices Offstage

Daisy (Henrietta Kaye) and Joseph (Harry McKee) mock the ways of their masters, Mrs. Entwhistle and Freddie.

I built the horse. I had a little studio down on Twenty-third Street and the first thing I did was model the horse from the drawing. I modeled it in clay, then I drew on the clay where I thought the seams should be. I took those seams and blew them up to the size I needed and I got the material, sort of a brown plush. I had a fellow sew them up for me; I just showed him what I wanted, and it worked. The horse had to roller skate and eat a hat, and the head was something I modeled and made out of papier mâché. Carol King had the front end and Edwin Denby, the back end. I delivered the horse one day and came down with my French horn (which I had bought for some purpose downtown), and I came in tooting a hunting horn. We brought the horse inside and everybody tried him out and liked him.

Orson was trying to get Hiram Sherman to fall into the orchestra pit. Hiram said he wouldn't do it. You know, that wasn't the kind of thing he would do—but Orson asked him to do anything. So I went, "Whoop!" like that, and did a flop and landed on my back in the orchestra pit. Everybody applauded and Orson said, "Mr. Baird, you're hired." I wasn't on the Project, I didn't get paid. I was a stagestruck kid.

BIL BAIRD, actor

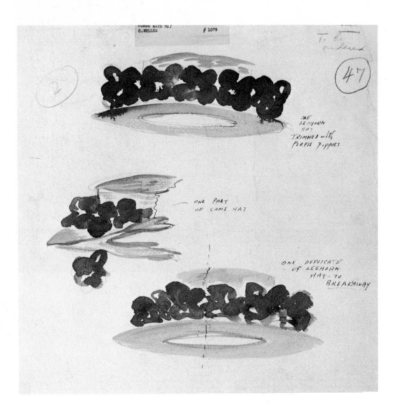

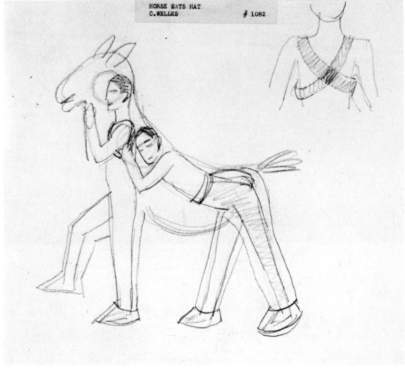

DOCTOR FAUSTUS

D OCTOR FAUSTUS was produced in five cities, but the Houseman-Welles production at the Maxine Elliott theatre stands out as a unique creation and one of the Federal Theatre's most dazzling productions. Originally scheduled as a two-week filler, it played to full houses for the first five months of 1937.

As with the previous year's *Macbeth*, Welles continued to prove that the classics of the Renaissance stage could be revived and could attract new audiences. He remarked in an interview at the time that, "The audience was fresh. It was not the Broadway crowd. . . . Even less was it the special audience one has learned to associate with classic revivals. One had the feeling every night, that here were people on a voyage of discovery in the theatre."

The play was filled with surprise and magic. Through the use of black velvet cylindrical curtains, trapdoors, and side and top lighting, people and objects suddenly appeared or disappeared. This show firmly established Abe Feder as the foremost lighting designer and demonstrated the importance of lighting in the theatre. The bare, thrust stage sharply contrasted with the lush costumes, which Welles had designed himself.

It was Welles' first leading role. John Houseman has written that, "the legend of the man who sells his soul to the devil in exchange for knowledge and power and who must finally pay for his brief triumph with the agonies of personal damnation was uncomfortably close to the shape of Welles' own personal myth. . . . There were moments when Faustus seemed to be expressing, through Marlowe's words, some of Orson's personal agony and private terror."

The stories of Welles' energy during each of his Federal Theatre plays are awesome and incredible. He inspired those around him and simply expected others to match his ability and enthusiasm. Fortunately, he was continuing to attract some of the finest actors, designers, and technicians in the Federal Theatre.

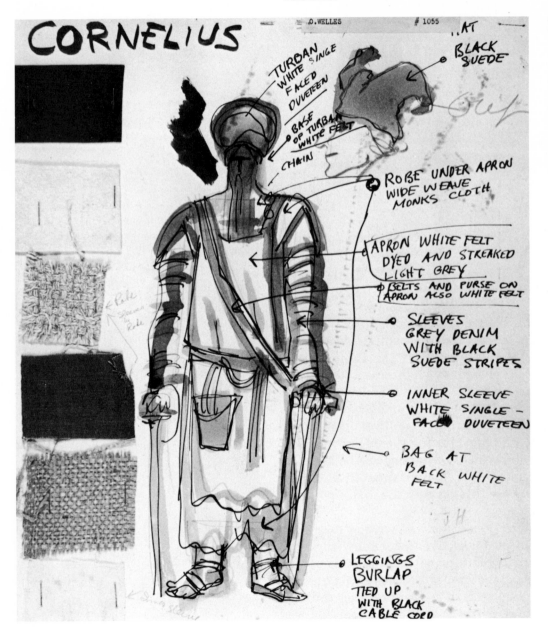

CORNELIUS

.O.WELLES   # 1055

..AT

BLACK SUEDE

TURBAN WHITE SINGLE FACED DUVETEEN

BASE OF TURBAN WHITE FELT

CHAIN

ROBE UNDER APRON WIDE WEAVE MONKS CLOTH

APRON WHITE FELT DYED AND STREAKED LIGHT GREY

BELTS AND PURSE ON APRON ALSO WHITE FELT

SLEEVES GREY DENIM WITH BLACK SUEDE STRIPES

INNER SLEEVE WHITE SINGLE-FACED DUVETEEN

BAG AT BACK WHITE FELT

LEGGINGS BURLAP TIED UP WITH BLACK CABLE CORD

At the end of the sequence, when the Devil's about to come for him, there was a glow from the side, which had a warm cast to it, and another wash. His friends leave him, and he stands center stage. All of a sudden the smoke pot started and out of the pipes, two pipes, came fingers of light. First this side, then that side, then this side—there were fingers of light. The smoke was filling up these fingers and they [his friends] stood parting there. Then as the mist came on, it was so blindingly bright, because of this battery of light, that as he stepped back, you didn't see him. A shaft picked him up through that mist and saw this face.

Now how to finish it. How did the Devil come to him? In the back, in the gloom, we had a container about three foot in diameter, and we had salamonica powder in there. And we had, along the side, some electric elements, and if you blew it, you'd see a flash of fire that would go up twenty feet. Through this mist, as this flash of fire occurred, BLACKOUT!

ABE FEDER, *lighting designer*

The main thing I remember is Jack Carter playing Mephistopheles. He was the most magnificent, dignified portrayal of evil I have ever seen, just beautiful. He was a black man genetically, but with such a fair skin. The black features just barely showed through, and the whole thing combined to give him a tremendous picture of dignity. Plus the fact that he was a beautiful man—tall, thin, beautiful.

WENDELL PHILLIPS, *actor*

Going into the Maxine Elliott during rehearsals was like going into the pit of hell: total darkness punctuated by stabs of light, trapdoors opening and closing to reveal bewildered stagehands or actors going up, down, and around in circles; explosions; properties disappearing in a clap of thunder; and on stage Orson, muttering the mighty lines and interspersing them with fierce adjurations to the invisible but omnipresent Feder. The only point of equilibrium in these midnight seances was Jack Carter, quiet, slightly amused, probably the only actor who ever played Mephistopheles without raising his voice. More subtle than the red flares and necromancy was the emphasis on an element of tragedy more in keeping with our age than that of a man being snatched away by the devil—that is, the search to lay hold on reality. Faustus, emerging out of darkness on the platform thrust boldly out into the audience, drew us into his imaginings of living in voluptuousness, of resolving all ambiguities, of being on earth as Jove is in the sky. Tragedy lay in seeing the Seven Deadly Sins from which rapture was expected reduced to the stature of puppets, lewd and nauseating, flopping about in the theatre box or at the feet of Faustus. Helen, in whose embrace Faustus hopes at last to get what he is paying for, is a distant masked figure.

HALLIE FLANAGAN, *from* Arena

The only woman's part in *Doctor Faustus* is a ghostly Helen of Troy. Paula Laurence, who had been the vamp in *Horse Eats Hat,* played the part with a mask—to emphasize the cold, pale aloofness of her beauty.

Jack Carter, who had played Macbeth in the 1936 Welles production, as Mephistopheles presents a show of the Seven Deadly Sins for Faustus. The puppets were designed and built by Bil Baird; his wife Cora was the voice for all Seven Sins.

VINTNER

Welles' view of the play dominated all parts of
the production. He designed the costumes himself, and the bold sketches reveal the characters as well as the costumes—the haughty car-
dinal, a distant Helen, a frightened friar, and the
drunken vintner.

THE POPE

Welles retained most of the comic subplot, with all its noise and fireworks. Here, two devils torment Wagner, Faustus' assistant.

In Faustus there's a clown part in the original and Orson cast the old man . . . [Harry McKee]. So he told me one day, "Go across the street and make a dance for him, 'cause I want him to have a dance." And I thought, what kind of dance? "You mean a Morris dance?" He said, "Yes, yes, yes—anything you want." So I had very vague ideas of what a Morris dance would be like, but I went over to the theatre across the street that was empty and where we could rehearse in the lobby, with a gramophone. At any rate, I tried to make a dance for him, and he did it as well as he could, but it didn't look at all right. I didn't know what to do about it, because I realized, after all, he's an old man. I was a young man. I could do some movements that would be formal of some sort, that looked like what they called chore-ography, but he couldn't. There was no use asking him to, so I said to him, "What could you do? What would you like to do?" And he said, "Well, I have this bauble, this little stick—I could play golf with it." I said okay.

So then we fixed it so that he would walk in a big square all over the stage and at the corners he'd either do a kind of a military thing that he invented . . . or play golf. Or

one time he spit on the floor and pretended that was a golf ball. It was really in the spirit of an Elizabethan clown. He understood that part and he could really do it.

So he did, in a performance. Of course the critics were all down on the WPA theatre anyway, but Stark Young, who was the great intellectual theatre critic, wrote an elaborate piece about this man as the real Elizabethan clown and how wonderful it was. And it was quite true! Stark Young was quite right. I thought so too—I was watching from the audience when he did it. I thought, "That's absolute-ly marvelous." I had nothing at all to do with it.

He'd been in the theatre all of his life, and it was the first time he'd gotten a big review. He was eighty-nine or something, and of course he was terribly happy. He'd always been in burlesque. He was that kind of funny man—an old fashioned fun-ny man. He'd never gotten a serious in-tellectual review. . . . We were all delighted with it, all the people who knew him, because he was such a sweet, adorable old man.

EDWIN DENBY, *playwright and actor*

IT CAN'T HAPPEN HERE

T HE NATIONWIDE, simultaneous openings of *It Can't Happen Here*, by Sinclair Lewis, were designed as a test of the FTP's organization and a demonstration of its resources. On October 27, 1936, twenty-two productions opened in eighteen cities: Birmingham, Boston, Bridgeport, Chicago, Cleveland, Denver, Detroit, Indianapolis, Los Angeles (two), Miami, Newark, New York (four), Omaha, San Francisco, Seattle, Tacoma, Tampa, and Yonkers. A production in Kansas City opened two weeks later, and nine of the units went on tour after the initial run. Before it was over, nearly 500 thousand people saw *It Can't Happen Here*; altogether, it ran for an equivalent of 260 weeks, or a five-year run. Unfortunately, the citizens of New Orleans and St. Louis were denied the chance to see the play. Local officials thought it too controversial; the career and death of Huey Long were still too fresh in the minds of some people.

Lewis, the first American novelist to win the Nobel Prize in literature, chose the Federal Theatre as a producer—despite commercial offers from Broadway—because of the national attention the play would receive. *It Can't Happen Here* had been published as a novel in 1935. The story of "Buzz" Windrip, a fascist politician elected to the U.S. Presidency, where he later establishes a dictatorship, proved to be a very popular best seller. Much of the book is focused on Doremus Jessup, a small-town editor who at first supports Windrip, but later joins the underground after a series of brutal acts by the dictator and his private military, the Corpos. MGM had quickly bought the movie rights, but a film was never made. (Lewis charged that the studio considered the topic too controversial.) During an FTP summer conference at Vassar in 1936, Francis Bosworth,

We want to do It Can't Happen Here because it is a play by one of our most distinguished American writers. We want to do it because it is a play about American life today, based on a passionate belief in American democracy. The play says that when dictatorship comes to threaten such a democracy, it comes in an apparently harmless guise, with parades and promises; but that when such dictatorship arrives, the promises are not kept and the parade grounds become encampments. We want to do It Can't Happen Here because, like Doremus Jessup and his creator, Sinclair Lewis, we, as American citizens and as workers in a theatre sponsored by the government of the United States, should like to do what we can to keep alive the "free, enquiring, critical spirit" which is the center and core of a democracy.

HALLIE FLANAGAN

The Yiddish productions in New York and Los Angeles had a special power because many in the audience were recent emigrés. In New York the part of the boy, David, was played by Sidney Lumet (both right and below). He later went to Hollywood to direct such films as *Long Day's Journey Into Night, The Pawnbroker,* and *Network.*

the director of the Play Bureau, suggested that the FTP produce the play nation-wide, and William Farnsworth, deputy national director of the FTP, asked that the openings be simultaneous.

In the ensuing three months, Lewis and John C. Moffitt, a Paramount scenarist, worked on a script. The first draft was a mess. Soon Hallie Flanagan and others were practicing "shuttle diplomacy" between Moffitt's and Lewis' rooms in the Essex House as the two men fought through the rewrites. Directors across the nation feared each day's mail would bring a new version of the scene they had just rehearsed. William Watts, the San Francisco director, spoke for many of his peers when he said, "The chief obstacle was the script itself—because of its hurried and superficial writing." The New York City directors asked if their productions might be delayed so that further revisions could be made after the "tryouts" in the other cities. Hallie Flanagan angrily responded that the FTP was a national theatre and New Yorkers were not prima donnas.

Her later judgment of the play in *Arena* is perhaps the best: "It was not as strong a play as it should be, nor did I think the production enhanced it. Yet the power of the idea was there." It was "the power of the idea" that caught the public's attention and sparked so much comment by the press. Over seventy-eight thousand lines were printed about the FTP productions before they even opened. Most of the publicity was favorable, but—with the 1936 election only weeks away—many critics of the New Deal saw the productions as campaign propaganda. The Indianapolis *News'* editorial comment was typical: "It can be regarded as one of the nation's most powerful agencies for the dissemination of propaganda." That a national theatre presenting controversial, topical issues could have a tremendous impact upon public opinion was not lost on Congress. Shortly after *It Can't Happen Here*, the Federal Theatre was faced with a substantial budget cut.

Lewis was not interested in doing just one production. But then out of desperation, Francis [Bosworth] said, "Look, you don't understand. We want to do this in as many productions and as many languages as we can, and opening on the same night." He jumped at it, of course. Bosworth came back to New York very excited about this whole project, and our publicity department inadvertantly, through some mistake, announced an opening date. We didn't have a word written. . . .

Lewis loved the theatre. He was theatrestruck. He had the bug. And he used to play all the characters. I have never seen anyone work like he worked. . . .

In New York, we opened on that same night, one production in Yiddish, two productions in English. I saw the first act in English, left, and saw the second act in Yiddish. The reason why the Yiddish business was so important was that we were beginning to get all the refugees from Austria and Germany—the Jewish refugees—at this time. At the Yiddish theatre opening, there were two or three people that fainted. They were identifying. . . .

H.L. FISHEL,
administrative assistant,
Play Bureau

It Can't Happen Here *was a dickens of a thing to do, because it had so many scenes. We had things pretty well planned by using jackknife stages that would roll in, complete with the set on it, and then another one would follow. One had the interior of the home of the characters, and that never changed—it just all of a sudden would swing into place. We had everything except the opening act, everything planned . . . finally the opening scene was written and sent to us, and where under the sun do you suppose it was? On a hilltop, at midday, somewhere in Vermont!*

FREDERICK STOVER, *Los Angeles designer*

IT CAN'T HAPPEN HERE   63

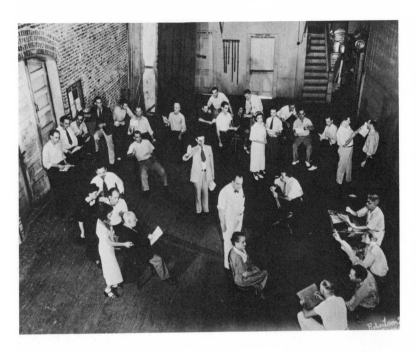

It was wonderful, what they did and no time at all to do it. We didn't have the last act until it was just about the time to start. Then it came, without who was to say what.

DOROTHEA LYNCH, *Florida state director*

Many of the productions were localized. In Birmingham (right), for instance, the production was done in the style of a southern political rally—noisy, festive, and bombastic. The theatre boxes were used for two scenes and the orators spoke to the audience, as well as the other actors. The Negro production in Seattle and the Spanish translation in Tampa (above right and left), emphasized the effect of a white dictatorship on minority groups.

I will never forget the series of things we went through. It was one thing after another, and finally (I was down there in Miami a good part of the time) . . . in came the darndest thing that was supposed to be distributed—a handbill to the audience—as though it had happened here. I read this thing, and I thought, "My God, if they go out with this, and somebody drops it outside the theatre, and somebody finds it, they'll say, 'Oh sure, it's communistic. This is the Federal Theatre just like we thought it was going to be.'" So, I said, "We're not going to use this. It would be absolutely suicidal to have this spread around and have the press get at it and have them think that it's done seriously and not as a parody." Well, it wasn't too long before we had a red-hot wire—"Destroy." We did in a hurry. But that was the way things went.

DOROTHEA LYNCH

Ted Browne as Doremus Jessup and Joe Staton as a Corpos sergeant in the Seattle production. Browne adapted *Lysistrata* and wrote *Natural Man* and *Go Down Moses* for the Federal Theatre.

I had one casting problem. It was to find the right person to do the part of the man who was jailed with the editor. The only person I felt was right for the part was a black man who was a very good actor. So I put him in the part. As a matter of fact, Mr. Lewis thought it intensified the dramatic effect of that particular scene to have the editor, who was something of an elitist, thrown into jail with a black man. [Lewis thought] it made the scene more valid to the audience than the way he had written it. He said that if he had thought of it that way, he would have written the part for a black man, a course I took out of necessity.

The other interesting thing about the production was that the actor I needed for the part of the bully was on the Jersey City project. I had arranged with Mrs. Flanagan to pull people from any of the local projects in New Jersey for this production. However the person I thought was right for the part was being "kicked off" the project because he did not have what the bureaucrats thought were the proper qualifications as a professional actor. As a matter of fact, it was the political chicanery that was rife in Mayor Hague's Jersey City project. Mayor Hague wanted to get some friend of his on this spot, a professional spot that paid a few dollars a week more, three or four dollars a week more, than the regular day laborer job. So I went to the top of the WPA in Newark and pleaded that I had to have this man and that his case be considered after the opening of It Can't Happen Here. It was agreed to delay the case. And after the opening there was no further effort to bounce him from the project. That man happened to be William Bendix.

LOUIS SIMON, *New Jersey director*

PRELIMINARY DRAWING
"MOON OF THE CARIBBES"

DESIGNER
PERRY WATKINS

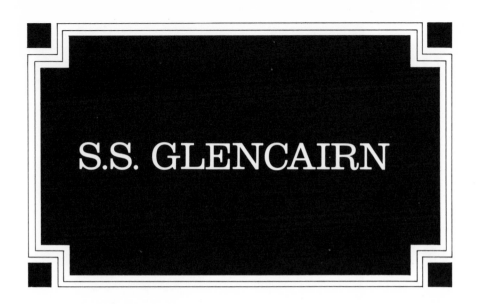

S.S. GLENCAIRN

WHEN EUGENE O'NEILL met Hallie Flanagan in Oregon in 1937, he was so impressed by the FTP's national program that he agreed to release his plays for the regular FTP royalty rate of fifty dollars a week. As a result of the 658 performances of his plays, O'Neill earned nearly five thousand dollars in royalties. Fourteen of his plays were mounted in twenty-seven cities, with a number of productions touring the country. *Ah, Wilderness!* was the play most frequently staged—nine separate productions with over twenty cities visited by tours. O'Neill was especially impressed by a marionette production of *The Emperor Jones* directed and produced by Ralph Chessé in San Francisco.

O'Neill's one-act plays were particularly well-suited to the peculiar strengths and weaknesses of the Federal Theatre. They called for a large number of actors in small parts, the settings were simple, and the dramatist well known. The life and language of the seamen no longer shocked audiences as they had twenty years earlier when the plays were first performed at the Provincetown Playhouse, but the drama was still convincing. In March 1938, all four sea plays—*Moon of the Caribbees, In the Zone, Bound East for Cardiff,* and *Long Voyage Home*—were produced in Philadelphia and New York under one bill entitled *S.S. Glencairn.*

O'Neill's sea plays were also produced as individual one-act plays. Chicago did *Long Voyage Home* in August 1937, with a young E.G. Marshall in the lead role. Walter Armitage came from New York to direct *Moon of the Caribbees* in New Orleans. The production there was localized by adding references to the New Orleans waterfront.

In the Philadelphia production of *S.S. Glencairn* Nick the Crimp was played by William Ogelsby.

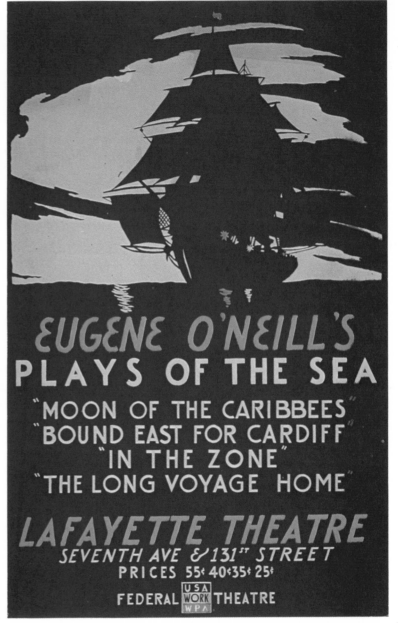

The WPA theatre projects have the opportunity to bring legitimate stage productions to every community in America, whether that community be rural or urban. The WPA units can present important plays before audiences that never before have seen an actual stage production. The possibilities in this respect are thrilling.

This program should try to find young talent, both on the footboards and at the typewriter. I hope those in charge will give every advantage to actors and writers who are just starting out. They should be encouraged and helped.

Heretofore the American idea of the theatre has been dictated by business considerations. Millionaires gave money for art museums, grand opera and archeological expeditions, but the theatre budget had to balance. Relatively little money went to the theatre. The WPA units are translating into action the fact that the government has an obligation to give a reasonable amount of encouragement and assistance to cultural undertakings.

EUGENE O'NEILL, *in a New York Times Magazine interview, November 22, 1936*

The director's problem in S.S. Glencairn is to tell the story of a hero, which is the crew of a ship, through the medium of individual histories of the members of that crew. The characters are extremely well and strongly drawn, and are in great contrast to one another. The casting should be done in order to bring out as great a variety of individuals as possible. Each play has its own mood, and O'Neill has supplied very simple, but strong atmospheric effects.

The problem of the first play, Moon of the Caribbees, is to give a picture of brutal and forceful action against a background of the beauty of the Caribbean sky and haunting melodies of the natives. The effect of moonlight and the music really play the leads of this play. It is important to get the actors to play in contrast to the scenic and auditory effects.

In the next play, In the Zone, the atmosphere is that of intense fear of men on a ship in the war zone expecting momentary death. The success of the play depends to a very large extent on the ability of the one actor called Plain Davis, to keep up this tension. He must have plenty of energy and nervous force.

In Bound East for Cardiff, O'Neill strengthens his play by another atmospheric effect: that of the regular sounding of the fog horn. This fog horn must be treated very carefully so that while it is insistent and always present, it doesn't drown out the lines. In this play O'Neill uses a contrast again with fine effect. He alternates passages of rough comedy with passages of quite tender emotion. The actor playing the part of the one who dies has a peculiarly hard job on his hands. He must play a rather long death scene full of reminiscences and past memories and yet keep our interest intact.

Playing opposite him is Driscoll, his pal. It was found the successful way to accomplish this scene was to eradicate from the mind of the actor playing Yank, all notions of the sadness of death or any idea of self-pity, and to express only the few moments of simple physical pain which he suffers. In the playing of same, Yank is having a perfectly happy time remembering the few good times he has had with his pal, Driscoll, and it is Driscoll who does the suffering, not Yank.

The last play, The Long Voyage Home, depends for its interest on its comedy and its irony. Here again the actor playing the lead, Ollie, must never get into his performance any suggestion that he is playing a tragedy. The other parts are also broadly and strongly drawn by O'Neill so that the average character actor can make a very successful job of them.

In mounting the play, it is important to throw away any romantic design of the ship. The most modern and simplest sets can be achieved by using the simple forms of structure in the average tramp steamer. They themselves simplify a striking beauty.

JAMES LIGHT, *in his director's report*

Jimmy Light first worked with O'Neill in 1917 after moving into an apartment above the Provincetown Playhouse. Over the next decade, they worked closely together on numerous Provincetown productions, including the first production of *S.S. Glencairn* in 1924. Light was also director of the Experimental Unit of the New York Federal Theatre Project, where he directed *Chalk Dust* and *Native Ground*.

At the Lafayette Theatre, the New York City Negro unit performed all four of the one-act plays. Perry Watkins, one of the few Negro designers in the thirties, did the sets and costumes. (Opposite page: *Moon of the Caribbees*. Top left: *In the Zone*. Top right and bottom left: *Long Voyage Home*. Bottom right: *Moon of the Caribbees*.)

Canada Lee (left, in the bed, and right, being restrained), in *Bound East for Cardiff*. Lee, a former prize fighter, played Banquo in the "voodoo" *Macbeth* and went on to star in *Native Son*.

Below: *Long Voyage Home*. Philadelphia.

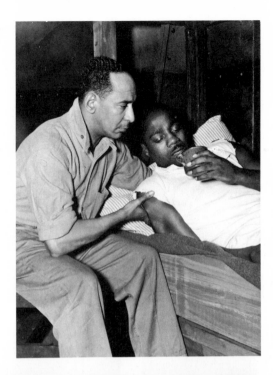

E.G. Marshall starred as Nick the Crimp in the Chicago production of *Long Voyage Home* (opposite page). On opening night the theatre was so hot they cut the last play in the series—*Long Voyage Home*.

The Court of Public Opinion

To **John Q. Citizen**, New York City

Greeting:

We Command You, That all business and excuses being laid aside, you appear and attend before The Court of Public Opinion, at the Biltmore Theatre, 261 West 47th Street, in the Borough of Manhattan, City of New York, on any evening excepting Sunday, at 8:45 P.M., to hear evidence in the case of Labor at a performance of

Injunction Granted!

And We Command You, further, that having heard the said evidence you forthwith testify to other persons, each and every one you meet, in the case of Labor therein presented.

L. S.

The Living Newspaper
of the
Federal Theatre
Works Progress Administration

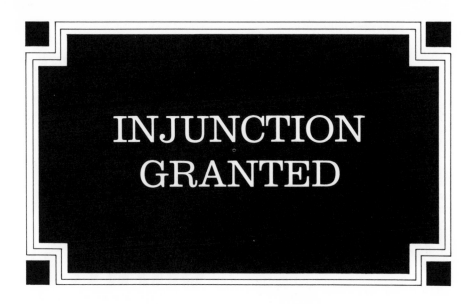

INJUNCTION GRANTED

I NJUNCTION GRANTED was the most quietly controversial of the living newspapers, partly because much of the dispute took place within the Federal Theatre. Though it played to full houses for three months, from July 24 to October 20, 1936, at the Biltmore Theatre on Broadway, memos were constantly exchanged between the producer and director and the FTP administrators about the show's merits and flaws.

The play traces the history of American labor from the days of indentured servants to the mid-thirties, emphasizing labor's "mistreatment" by the courts, who are the dupes of the industrial bosses. In scene after scene, labor's attempts to organize are repeatedly frustrated through legal technicalities, until at the end the court rules the Guffey Act, the NRA, the Labor Relations Act, and the Minimum Wage Law either unconstitutional or inapplicable. The play ends with a speech by John L. Lewis and his ringing pronouncement, "Organized labor in America accepts the challenge of the overlords of steel."

Hallie Flanagan thought the production was "bad journalism and hysterical theatre." In a memo after the opening night performance, she wrote, "The production seems to me special pleading, biased, an editorial, not a news issue. Whatever my personal sympathies are I cannot, as custodian of federal funds, have such funds used as a party tool. That goes for the Communist party as well as the Democratic party. To show the history of labor in the courts is appropriate; to load that document at every turn with insinuation is not appropriate. The production, in my opinion, lacks a proper climax, falling back on the old cliche of calling labor to unite in the approved agit-prop manner . . ." Of

Capital or Labor? Class conflict is a demagogue's delight. Here, one not only talks out of both sides of his mouth, but also dresses the part for each group. Norman Lloyd as the clown orchestrates the applause.

course the Communists also objected: the play offered unionization rather than revolution as the solution.

Morris Watson, an early organizer of the Newspaper Guild, supervised the whole living newspaper unit, and Joseph Losey was his director. They argued against the administrator's complaints and interference, refused to change the production significantly, and finally left the Project when *Injunction Granted* closed.

Losey had studied in Russia for eight months in 1935, and his stage design, choreography, and lighting for this production reflected Russia's new theatre techniques. This experimental style seemed to influence the young stage manager of the show, Nick Ray, in his later career as a film director (*Rebel Without a Cause, They Live By Night,* and *Johnny Guitar*).

Virgil Thomson composed the musical score, using lots of horns and bells for the production. The play was indeed noisy, if not hysterical. In fact, during the first dress rehearsal the noise was so great that neighbors complained and the police burst into the theatre with guns drawn.

SCENE: *Jennings vs. Hearst*

VOICE OF LIVING NEWSPAPER: The case of Dean S. Jennings, newspaper man. . . . (*Lower ring marquee from flies. Referee enters 5, stands at 3. Hearst enters 1 wearing boxing gloves, straw hat and carrying stool, and sits. Jennings enters 2, wearing gloves, carrying stool, sits. Both wear fighting trunks and shoes.*)

REFEREE: Ladies and gentlemen, a fight to a finish. In this cunnah we have Dean Jennings, the pride of the Newspaper Guild A.C. and in this cunnah, William Randolph Hearst, Champion of the Non-Collective Bargaining Athletic Association.

VOICE OF THE LIVING NEWSPAPER: (*As men walk to center of ring.*) Both men are in the pink, folks, rarin' to go. They can't seem to wait for the bell. (*As the men walk to the center on the Referee's call for their instructions, Referee puts patronizing arm around Hearst, and shakes his finger vigorously into Jennings' face, warning him apparently that he is not to mistreat his man. Both men go to the corners. They bend their knees, holding imaginary ropes. Bell rings, and they come to the center of the ring. As the Voice of the Living Newspaper calls the blows, Hearst leads with a left, freezes with his glove outstretched. Jennings tries an uppercut and holds his hand in the air at termination of the punch, and so on through the fight. After throwing a punch, each man holds it until his next punch. The bell.*)

VOICE OF THE LIVING NEWSPAPER: *There they go!* Hearst leads with a left. . . . he misses. . . . Jennings tries an uppercut. . . . he misses. . . . Hearst leads with left. . . . he misses. . . . Jennings tries an uppercut. . . . HE SOCKS HIM! HE'S DOWN! The National Labor Board orders Jennings reinstated. (*Referee seats himself on Hearst's stool, fanning himself with the latter's straw hat.*)

REFEREE: One, two, three, four, five, six . . . (*Looks into hat band.*) Six and seven-eighths, seven, eight, nine. . . . (*Looks around appealingly for help.*) Get up Randolph — eleven, twelve, thirteen. (*At "thirteen" Richberg enters 4, wearing name sign around his neck, and stands at 3 giving the Referee instructions.*)

VOICE OF THE LIVING NEWSPAPER: Wait a minute! Something's goin' on here. Richberg just entered the ring with a message. (*The Referee, having listened to Richberg, comes apologetically forward to the audience.*)

REFEREE: Pardon me, folks, that was a mistake. The case is re-opened. We gotta fight all over again. (*Referee rushes over to Hearst and props him up ready to fight again. The Loudspeaker resumes calling the punches as before. The same routine as the first fight is gone through, but with the Loudspeaker much more exited, pace much more rapid.*)

VOICE OF THE LIVING NEWSPAPER: All over again, folks. Slips don't count. . . . There they go! Hearst tries a left but he misses. Jennings tries an uppercut to his face, but he misses. Hearst leads with his chin. . . . Jennings lets go with an uppercut—HE SOCKS HIM. (*Hearst falls.*)

VOICE OF THE LIVING NEWSPAPER: (*Continuing.*) HE'S DOWN! Here comes the decision, folks. We'll know in just a moment! (*Richberg runs in with the decision, and the Referee lifts the hand of the unconscious Hearst.*)

REFEREE: The winnah! (*Blackout.*)

The musicians had a slightly different setup from the theatre. The musicians' salary was the same as everybody else's. I think it was $26.84 a week, something like that, on account of the particular contract that had been made with the musicians' union for that amount of money. They only served a certain number of hours and that number of hours was smaller than the number of hours that your stagehands and actors were serving, so that you could run a Federal Theatre play with the same actors night after night with understudies, but you didn't change the cast any more than normally. But the musicians had to be staggered, because their services amounted to about two-thirds of what everybody else's was. For a body of string players or a large percussion group that was quite easy. If you have one piccolo or English horn or something like that he is a little hard to stagger on the two-thirds basis; but, anyway, we managed it by having plenty of rehearsals beforehand. The wonderful thing about the Federal Theatre is that since it was in its basic motivation relief for unemployed artists, it was desirable to hire as many as you could, so that you could have enormous casts and enormous orchestras and big choruses and all that. You didn't have to economize as the commercial theatre does.

The cast for the living newspaper was quite large. Morris Watson was director of the [living newspaper unit] and he had caused Injunction Granted to be written—I don't remember who wrote it—and he had engaged Joe Losey to direct it, and then Joe asked me if I would write music for this, and I said, "Sure." The music was almost entirely percussive. I had an orchestra of sixteen, I think; and they were all percussion players. They could play everything you could think of. There were sixteen snare drums sitting there, sixteen bass drums, sixteen bronx cheers, sixteen slapsticks, everything. You could make lots of noise and amusement—and for overture and some dramatic moments I acquired from some warehouse or technical store downtown three different sizes of electrical sirens so that for the overture we would turn on one, then two, then three, then let them all die down. That was the overture. That placed us in the industrial world, you see, which is what the play was about. There is no point in making Mother Machree or sentiment—what you wanted to do was use industrial sounds. Also with a script that jumps about in tiny little pieces it is valuable to punctuate everything, so I used those percussion instruments to separate one thing from another or to hit something on the nose or to salt the whole thing up. I think there were something like 496 music cues.

VIRGIL THOMSON, *composer*

I saw Injunction Granted from out front, then I saw Losey the next day and said, "Joe, pretty good show, but couldn't we take that old judge who can hardly crawl on the stage and get him out of there, replace him. He's too old, he's not articulating that clearly."

Losey almost hit me; he was that angry. He rose up to his full height and said, "That's Fuller Mellish. Don't ever say anything about him."

Fuller Mellish was just what we were set up to do. That dear old man had toured this country in Shakespeare shows from way back when, with [Sir Henry] Irving. He was an old man; he was on actor's welfare. This was what we were there for, and Losey was practically saying, "If you don't know that—to make a job for Fuller Mellish, with everybody in the cast helping him get up dark steps and putting him up to say 'Injunction Granted' twice— what is the matter with you." This was true, and it was a very good first lesson.

ESTHER PORTER LANE, *assistant stage manager*

The Russian influence of Meyerhold and Okhlopkov on Losey is apparent in the set design. The platforms, runways, and steps offered ten separate acting areas that could be individually lighted. This fluid space could be used for sharp contrasts from space to space or light to dark, or for smooth transitions from an empty stage to a crowded one. With this flexible stage, Losey was able to break the action into 100 separate scenes using 125 players.

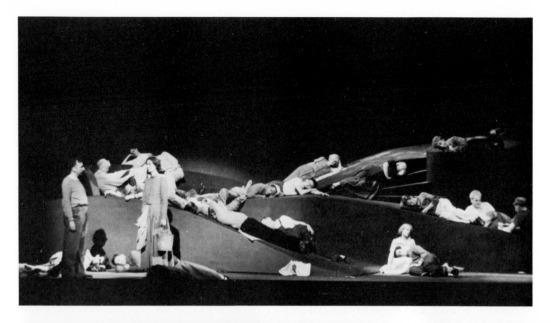

The pantomime of the actors' rhythmic, patterned movements showed another influence of the European stage on Losey, and was used to capture the tedious repetition in the modern industrial workers' life. The tempo of the movement and the sound were dramatically increased to show the strain the workers had to bear. Their collective force is implicit in their grouping together.

About the time of rehearsals I went to the circus that was in New York. The circus used to play Madison Square Garden and then it would go out to Brooklyn. I went out to Brooklyn to see it, because it was under a tent.

I knew that Joe was going to be doing Injunction Granted. I seem to have read the script, I believe, and there was nothing that was really too exciting I wanted to do in it. As I watched the circus I got an idea, and I went to Joe and suggested that I perform as a clown all through it, commenting on the action and on the script. He was receptive to that idea and permitted me to develop it almost in an improvisational sense. . . .

It was totally pantomime; I never spoke a word. I did learn some magic tricks for it. The set Losey had worked out was a series of ramps that had a continuation, almost like a freeway, but went from down to up then down and up again. In one area there was a turret or a great well, and I lived in that. There was a trap door and I'd pop out of it, and in there I had stashed all my magic tricks.

Somebody would want a higher wage and somebody would say "No" or whatever it was, and I would pop out and maybe have a big cigar, one of those trick cigars, and make some comment. Or I'd pull a bouquet out of my sleeve, you know that old corny trick, and present it to somebody—that sort of thing. Balloons would appear from nowhere and so on. I had a little piano I could carry, one of those children's pianos, and I would play little tunes on it as I galumphed along.

Also I would just do pantomime. My costume was a pair of corduroys with all sorts of patches, sneakers, a turtleneck sweater, and a long patchwork coat down to about the calf. So it was pantomimic commenting, both on those who you might call Capital, and also commenting on Labor too. Both. He would make a comment. He would almost be the objective observer. As if to say, "Well, you're right," or "You're right." I shouldn't use the word "right"—there's no right or wrong here—but it would be a comment either favorable or unfavorable. He was indiscriminate.

NORMAN LLOYD, actor

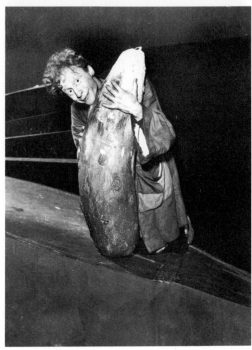

Mopey Dick and the Duke, cartoon characters of the period, comment upon a speech by President Hoover, in which he declares, "Immediate need for the unemployed is the immediate need of the hour." Using comic-strip characters to undercut the action points out the pomposity and inadequacy of most official pronouncements about labor problems. This mocking of the government, regardless of political party, may have contributed to the FTP administrators' dislike of the play.

Because Processional is a play of sharp contrasts in mood and style, a scene of "slapstick" vaudeville following immediately upon a scene of realistic or poetic intensity, the function of music is necessarily varied. In general the music is used to soften these changes, to build up moods or to satirize them.

The music falls into two general categories—thematic and background. There are three main themes. The miners' Jazz Band forms the basis for one of the main themes. The tune is in the jazz style of 1925; corny, raucous, "hotcha." The tune is introduced by the miners' band on stage; it is repeated by the orchestra in succeeding scenes as comment on the action. In this development it satirizes the Man in the Silk Hat, scares the soldiers, makes the Sheriff lose his temper. The orchestra is unseen and the music is broadcast on stage through loudspeakers. This theme is used throughout the first act and for the last part of the third act.

During the first act, two supplementary themes are introduced, one for Sadie Cohen, and one for Jim Flimmens. The music develops along with the characters. The music is used in Wagnerian fashion to signal entrance or mention of the two characters, but more generally because of the emotional significance inherent in the themes. These themes are present underneath the love scenes, the man hunt, and as a carry-over between other scenes.

The second main division of music is background music which is contrapuntal to the action on stage; that is, it gives the mood of what the characters are thinking in opposition to what they may be saying, or satirizes the entire action. This type of music is used in the third scene of the first act, the KKK scene and two of Philpotts' scenes.

CHARLES D. FRANZ,
head of the music department,
from Earl Robinson's notes

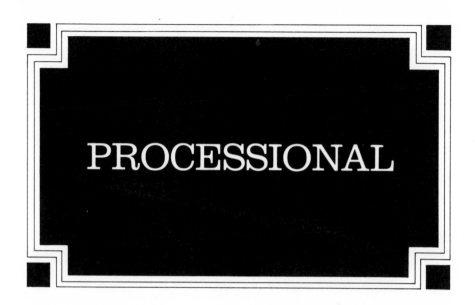

PROCESSIONAL

J OHN HOWARD LAWSON'S "jazz drama of protest" was revived by the Federal Theatre twelve years after the original Theatre Guild production of *Processional* in 1925. The Guild production, which had favorably impressed some of the audience and reviewers and deeply irritated others, also aroused a controversy that extended into the Letters to the Editor section of the New York papers. Two weeks after the opening, the Guild scheduled a debate on the merits of the play.

Lawson, in the preface to the published play, explained that he had "endeavored to create a method which shall express the American scene in native idiom, a method as far removed from the older realism as from the facile mood of Expressionism." This new technique he described as "essentially vaudevillesque in character," with a "staccato burlesque" rhythm "carried out by a formalized arrangement of jazz music." The actual production was as confusing to read about as it was startling to see.

Mordecai Gorelik, who designed the earlier Guild production, remembers that "the garish backdrops of the cheap burlesque stage were the scenic inspiration for this cartoon fantasy, which related the events of a mine strike in terms of jazz. Miners, soldiers, the Ku Klux Klan, an agitator, a Man in a Silk Hat, a reporter—all took part in a furious merry-go-round, proving Lawson's thesis that "the Twentieth Century is exciting to the point of chaos."

Lem Ward directed the FTP's *Processional*, Manuel Essman designed the set, and Earl Robinson composed the musical score. Their production, which reflected the more somber mood of the thirties, emphasized content and subject,

George Mathews as Dynamite Jim.

and took an excerpt from the author's preface as its philosophical keynote:

Buried under the hokum of advertisements, headlines, radio speeches, there is a genuine inner necessity, a sense of direction. What is this key and meaning? What does the future hold beside the indefinite prolongation of human life by glandular treatment and the total annihilation of it in the eagerly expected Next World War?

Perhaps this time, the struggle of Dynamite Jim, a West Virginia coal miner, against the forces of Capitalism, and the story of his disillusionment, capture, and mutilation, struck a more responsive note with Federal Theatre viewers and reviewers who could now "recognize a true portrait of America."

The Capitalist and the Law-and-Order Sheriff resemble street-corner agit-prop.

The FTP's set could have taken three forms, according to the designer:

One was to reflect the cross-section of rural America in the early 1920s, combining the historical and the burlesque through simple drops and curtains. The second was to make coal the central theme and motivating force of the production. Thirdly, the choice of designing the show in a theatrical and stylized form, setting it up strictly as a rostrum for action. However, none of these separately conveyed the authentic realism implied in the script. It was only after working out these approaches that it was decided the present production would have to be three dimensions in design. Around a single construction composed of a platform and two towers were finally set additional pieces and forms to change the physical character of the various scenes."

MANUEL ESSMAN, *set designer*

After her performance as Sadie Cohen, Ruth Gilbert became the most discussed of Project actresses; she was even approached by the movies.

The first [play] I really got a chance to work on was a revival of John Howard Lawson's *Processional*. Lem Ward . . . was a marvelous director, and he liked my background. He had very different ideas: to put the orchestra down under stage and not be seen. And by God, he worked it out! We had an eight-piece orchestra, way down—hell, you couldn't see what was happening whatsoever, but it worked out so that the stage manager would give a signal for some music to start. There were actually songs—maybe one song—that were accompanied by this orchestra down under stage. There was a conductor down there ready with the lights. The light would go out, and he'd start . . . I don't think it had ever been done before. Lem just didn't want the audience to see the musicians. As a matter of fact, I think he raked the stage a little bit front so that they'd be closer.

EARL ROBINSON, *composer*

The author, in attempting to find American roots for a theatrical style, has utilized the technique of vaudeville, burlesque, as well as the serious drama and even musical comedy.

The play is essentially a conflict of two philosophies which were prevalent in the post-war period in the United States—idealism as against cynicism. It is the cynicism of the Mencken school in conflict with the idealism of certain Utopian labor leaders and social workers, which is represented in the clash of the characters, with each other, with their environment and with the economic and social conditions of the time.

The author, being a poet who uses the colloquial poetry of America, does not present his characters as real people in the sense of their being naturalistically treated. Therefore, we find, from time to time, a character expressing some deep-seated and rich truth which superficially seems to be out of relation to that character's understanding and background. Here the style of production must clarify by showing that the character is in essence a type rather than a specific individual. In other places the play suddenly turns vaudevillesque, so that the characters speak directly to the audience and seem to step out of the realistic treatment of previous scenes. It is the intention of the author to make use of all the theatrical means to make his point.

The director's problem is one of making the style of his "vaudeville" serve that purpose and not become obtrusive and a thing in itself . . . .

LEM WARD, *director,*
from his report on the play

"ELLA"

"DANCER"

RUN, LITTLE CHILLUN

THE NEGRO UNIT in Los Angeles had been quiet for nine months prior to the production of *Run, Little Chillun*. Anxious to get back into production, a committee was organized to read plays. On the shelves of the FTP play department, they discovered Hall Johnson's *Run, Little Chillun*, which had been produced in 1933 in New York City. Since it incorporated dancing, singing, and dramatic action, and because Johnson himself was in Los Angeles, it seemed like the ideal play. When Clarence Muse agreed to join the unit as "guest director," they had the firm directorial hand necessary for a successful production.

The play, which dramatized the conflict between Christianity and a more primitive religion, called for a large cast, lots of music, and sets that ranged from city street scenes to woodland rituals to storefront churches. The female lead—a tempestuous Delilah-figure called Sulamai—was sought after by most black actresses in the area. Muse picked Florence O'Brien, a virtual unknown whom he spotted walking across the stage during rehearsals. With the help of Nelson Baumé and Frederick Stover for sets, Dale Wasserman on lights, and Jester Hairston directing the choir, Muse put together a *Run, Little Chillun* that packed houses until the FTP was closed a year later. Because of the success of the Los Angeles production, the play was produced in San Francisco under the direction of Jester Hairston, as a WPA exhibit in the Golden Gate Exposition of 1939.

Muse had established himself as a talented singer, actor, writer, and director before 1938. After graduating from Dickinson University with a degree in law, he had performed in over 200 plays and films and had formed his own theatre com-

pany in New York and in the South. Following the production of *Run, Little Chillun*, Muse continued his singing and acting in the motion picture and television industries, chalking up roles in *Huckleberry Finn* and *Porgy and Bess*. His music credits include such compositions as "Liberty Road," "Lazy Rain," and his famous "When It's Sleepy Time Down South," the theme song for Louis Armstrong. Muse retired from show business many years ago, but he still responds to studio calls. Most recently he portrayed the prophet in *Buck and the Preacher*, and the shoeshine man in *Car Wash*.

Before Muse joined the Federal Theatre in Los Angeles, the black unit had been repeating the productions of other cities and searching for an identity. The success of *Run, Little Chillun* established a visible pride and self-assurance in the unit. Despite the low admission prices, the production made enough money to pay for new equipment, sets, and costumes for all of the Los Angeles units, and gave the black unit equal billing with the others. For a brief moment a vibrant and successful Negro theatre was created in Los Angeles.

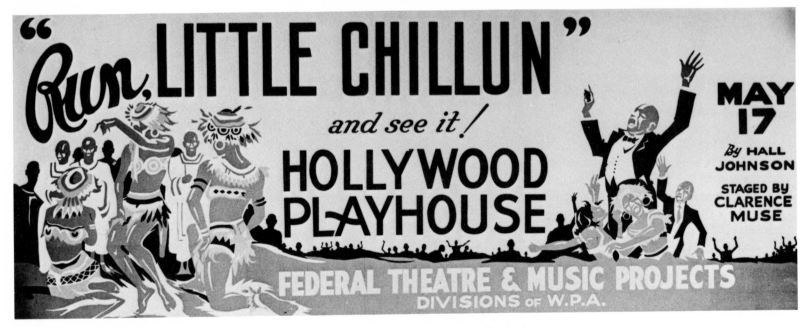

I came in and helped out [on Run, Little Chillun*] because I had a great many friends involved in it, and I knew Clarence Muse slightly. I remember the production very precisely, from moment to moment. It was one of those that was more fun to work with because of the vitality that was being poured out on that stage.*

DALE WASSERMAN, *stage manager*

In the great scene in the forest there, where the Pilgrims are going, . . . we got to talking about the scenic effects. So we developed the idea of having the lower part of a tremendous tree, like up in the Red Hills here in California, and the roots all raised up out of the ground, some of them six, eight inches in diameter. And these people would pass around, down through the tree, around over these tremendous roots. It established the whole "earth" quality of what was happening with the Pilgrims.

Well, we played around with that several weeks. You know, we didn't have no millionaires down there telling you how much money we was going to have. We was on the WPA; money was flowing for good. So we took our time and fooled 'round with that. After while, we created that scene with 165 people passing before the audience while it was on.

CLARENCE MUSE

Sulamai introduces Jim into the rites of the moon-worshipping New Day Pilgrims.

I'd been sick and tired of hearing those real crappy storms. That bothered me for a while. So we were up on the boulevard one day, Baumé and I—and we found a guy that would do it. We had him build us a drum eight feet tall, six feet wide, and where in the devil he got those pins, I never did know. He was an Italian from the old school in Rome, and he said, "I know what you're working, I'll tell you how you fix this drum. . . ." Anyhow, we took this big drum, so that when you hit it, the thunder rang just the same as that . . . "boommmmmmmmmm, boommmmmmmmmmmm." And then the rafters of the theatre shook, and everybody in the theatre started putting their coats up, "cause they know they're gonna get wet"—that's how very real it was.

CLARENCE MUSE, director

[Ed Sullivan] failed to mention how my set designer, who had a very unique approach, came into the picture . . . Nelson Baumé, a little Frenchman from Buffalo, New York, came to me and said, "Is there any way in the world that I can get on your project, Mr. Muse, as you are just the guest director here?" And after a few conversations with him, after he brought me a couple drawings, I said "Yes."

I remember he'd lay the sets down; I'd take a look at them. This was a long time before we even started a rehearsal of the dramatic part, because we took on the music first. The amazing thing is that this same man ended up being the first set designer for the Ed Sullivan Show—stayed there five years. Then I believed what [Sullivan, who had compared Run, Little Chillun to the Moscow Art Theatre] said about the show being good.

CLARENCE MUSE

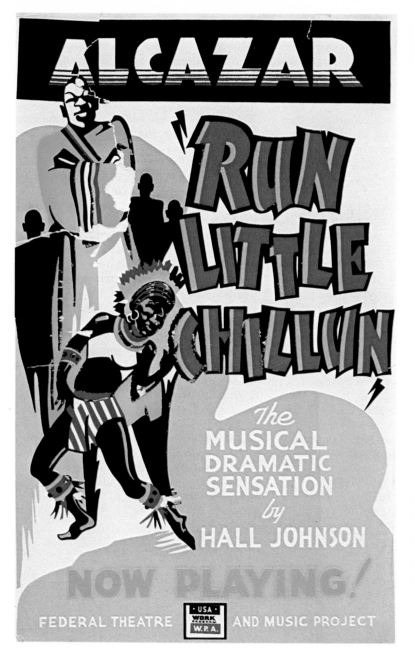

I tried to keep it as close to the New York version as possible, because I was so closely related to Hall Johnson, that I even tried to emulate him, in his thinking, especially where the Negro folklore was concerned. When we put the show together in New York, we worked practically seven months of 1932. We were all broke (those were Depression days), and there were about 125 blacks in the cast, all experienced show people. . . .

We went to the Elks Hall on 138th Street. The janitor there permitted us to come in and rehearse out of the cold weather. He just loved those old spirituals. And we rehearsed all day long. Nobody had any money to speak of. When it was time to eat lunch, we'd take up a collection, everyone contributing whatever he had, nickel, dime or whatever. The women went out on Eighth Avenue and bought vegetables and meat and came back and cooked it. The janitor let them use the stove downstairs. . . . When the cooking committee was ready with the lunch, they would call us and all 125 of us would go down to eat. It was a tremendous thing to see; all those actors out of work, but determined to put Hall Johnson's play together, because it was so real, so much a part of our culture.

We rehearsed till Hall Johnson returned from his concert tour. By the time he returned, we had the complete show together, lines, music, dances and all. We had done it so many times that each of us was an actual part of the play, the community in the play and the church scene. When Hall contacted a white producer from downtown, the producer had a complete show.

When we, Juanita and I, were putting the church scene together, we'd say to the people, "When you go to your particular church on Sunday, whatever denomination it is, if you see anything, any action or bit of business you think could fit into this church scene, take it down and bring it in on Monday." And so, every piece of business we put into that church scene, someone saw or heard in their particular church. It was, in truth, authentic Negro folklore of the thirties. We put nothing in there that would or should offend any denomination. It was not a Flip Wilson church scene; it was the real thing. In those days a Broadway show rehearsed a drama five weeks and a musical show four weeks. But the producer who took Run, Little Chillun to Broadway had it all rehearsed for him. He just said, "I'll take it." All he had to do was buy the sets and put us in them. He did not have to spend a month rehearsing us at all.

JESTER HAIRSTON, *choir director*

Similar to the Pilgrims' meeting is the last scene in the Baptist church when Jim returns to the fold. The Baptists work themselves into an ecstatic frenzy . . . destroyed only by Sulamai's death.

[Baumé] said, "I was looking at the rehearsal of that church sequence. I'd like for you to give me the authority to work out the whole technicolor treatment of wardrobe . . . . I can make it look like a quilt." And he did, with the different kind of colors of waists and garments and all. So when you looked on the scene from the audience (and the elevation was raised so it would go up), you could see everybody in that church sequence. It was just like looking at a quilt. He designed each and every bit of wardrobe for each person in that scene.

CLARENCE MUSE

Jim's choice between Ella (Los Angeles, upper right) and Sulamai (Los Angeles, right, and San Francisco, above) is also a choice between what traditions to follow—the Hope Baptists or the pagan New Day Pilgrims.

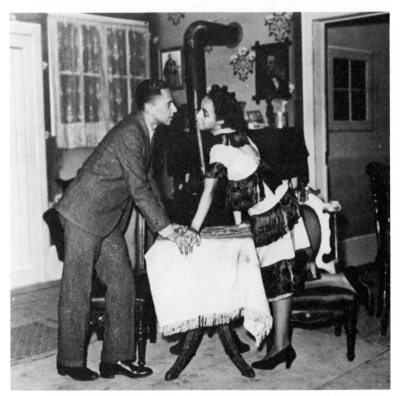

A young man from back East named Izenour . . . was the lighting man that I located on the job. He did a lot of creative things. For example, we had a scene in the middle of the stage, middle of the drama, where the boy and the girl have quite a little spat . . . . The tremendous impact of the situation was, "I'm going to do it with or without you."

Now they're leaning over a little marble table, and right then and there, here I come with some of my gag. I said, "Izenour, is there any way you can blow a hole in that piece of marble table there and put a baby spot up under it, so that when she says "with or without you" the light hits her right in the face and we'll get a close-up?" And he says, "Will do." And he did. Sensational to the audience.

That same Izenour is the man who created the console—a control thing like an organ. It's still being used in all the studios.

CLARENCE MUSE

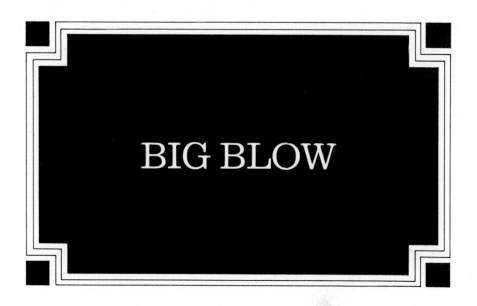

BIG BLOW

BIG BLOW, a roaring melodrama about Yankee farmers, Florida "Crackers," and hurricanes, was one of the big coast-to-coast hits in the FTP's final season. The play is a good example of the standard fare of many FTP units: Only a small percentage of the Federal Theatre's productions were "social dramas"; more often they were comedies and melodramas. *Big Blow* satisfied Hallie Flanagan's guidelines that the FTP produce new plays with social themes and regional settings, but its real appeal was its lovely romance, violence, and suspense. The plot line is clear and the characters are durable, dramatic types.

Wade Barnett, a young Nebraska farmer, moves to Florida for his mother's health. He finds that he must contend not only with the desert soil, but with the intense hostility of his neighbors as well—an illiterate, suspicious crowd who dislike "furriners" from the "up-country." Bugs and thieves destroy Wade's crops, but his real trouble comes when he defends a Negro who has stopped the villain from raping the young ingenue. Wade and the Negro are saved from a sure lynching during a Holy Roller meeting by a hurricane. Wade's log cabin— like the brick house of the third little pig—withstands the wind and allows him to demonstrate true neighborliness. The play ends with the villain dead, the community chastised, and the hero rewarded.

Big Blow opened in New York in November of 1938, two years after a major hurricane had devastated the Florida coast. Following a successful New York run, the FTP units in Boston, Chicago, and Los Angeles produced the play in the spring of 1939. Some northern critics found the characters unrealistic, but the

With the hurricane threatening outside, enemies become fast friends. Amelia Romano is the young heroine holding the window shut, and Doe Doe Green, the black servant who moments before faced a noose, is now "one of us." E. G. Marshall was listed in the cast, but ended up as a Cracker understudy.

author, Theodore Pratt, said, "It took me nearly two years of continual research—inland, as far from the winter tourist coasts as I could get, drinking bad whiskey with the Crackers, farming with them, 'gobbing' wads of snuff, going to cockfights and Holy Roller meetings, and living through two hurricanes—to get the material for *Big Blow*." Nevertheless, the play reinforced northern stereotypes of the South, and the play was not produced in its home state nor anywhere else in the South.

In Big Blow, I was playing this young, little, poor girl from the Florida swamps, an orphan of fifteen, taken care of by the old Negro servant. During the course of the play one of the other men tries to attack me, and Doe Doe Green . . . who was playing the part of Clay, the Negro servant, protects me and has to hit this man. A black man hitting a white man brought only one consequence, you know—they were out to lynch him. I protect him: At one point during the performance I ran to him and threw my arms around him. Now that embrace got a lot of flak, although Dodie was delighted; a lot of his friends, an awful lot of blacks, came to the theatre for the first time because of [that scene]. There were occasional hisses from the audience, but I refused to change it, because it seemed eminently right to me.

AMELIA ROMANO, *actress*

Producer Morris Ankrum had some of the FTP's finest technical help. Sam Leve designed the set, Mary Merrill the costumes, and Abe Feder the lighting.

I used two units and a car driven on. The two units could get together. First one unit is over here and one unit is over there. Then both units are together, which makes the set. The blow comes, the storm comes, and the whole house seems to shake and fall apart. (We had a fulcrum, and a guy stepped on it.) The two units came apart. It was very exciting to see.

SAM LEVE, *set designer*

The Chicago and Los Angeles productions emphasized the melodramatic tensions of the play.

114   BIG BLOW

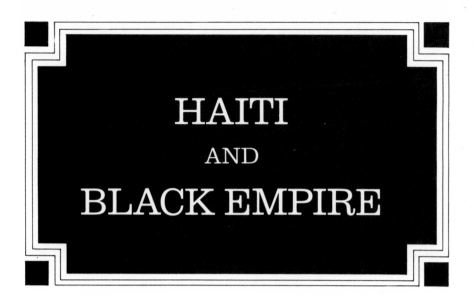

HAITI
AND
BLACK EMPIRE

B LACK UNITS throughout the country searched for new plays that would reflect the strength and power of blacks in history and especially give their actors the challenging dramatic roles they were hungry for. Seattle and New York City had produced plays on John Henry, and the Birmingham unit produced *Great Day*, a musical panorama of early African history. Playwrights like Abram Hill and Hughes Allison drafted plays about the African heritage of American blacks and the early days of slavery. A particularly appealing topic was the stormy history of the black rebellion against France in Haiti, and two plays produced by the Federal Theatre were written on the life of Henri Christophe: *Black Empire* by Christine Ames and Clarke Painter, and *Haiti* by William DuBois, a reporter for the *New York Times*.

Actually, southerner DuBois' original script focused on the evils of miscegenation, but New York director Maurice Clark was able to rewrite enough of it to bring forth the underlying dramatic story of the struggle for racial identity and self-determination for black Haiti. The plot revolves around Odette Boucher, ostensibly a French woman who does not know her real father is a black aide to Toussaint L'Ouverture. When she learns the truth about her heritage, she must decide whether to betray General Christophe—and her father who is a spy—to the French or to stay quiet and implicitly join their side. The conflict made for gripping theatre. The play was produced in the spring and summer of 1938 at the Lafayette Theatre, where over seventy-seven thousand people saw it. James R. Ullman (who later authored *The White Tower* and *River of the Sun*) was the producer, and Leonard de Paur composed the musical score. After its Harlem

Alvin Childress, Louis Sharp, and Rex Ingram as Jacques, L'Ouverture, and Christophe. All three actors continued Broadway careers after the success of *Haiti*.

run, the show toured a week in Boston and then inspired a subsequent production by the black unit in Hartford, Connecticut.

The same historical period inspired *Black Empire*, about the collapse of Henri Christophe's dream empire by the forces of voodoo, which represent the ignorance and savagery that Christophe had spent a lifetime trying to erase. The problems of political reform and popular superstition that continue to trouble Haiti are more important here than in the DuBois play. Chosen as one of the first Los Angeles productions, *Black Empire* opened in March of 1936 and played in a number of the area theatres, including the Hollywood Playhouse and the Greek Theatre, until July 1936. The FTP playreaders had worried about whether the voodoo would seem unbelievable or too alien to audiences, but it was a well-received and popular show.

Two years later the small, excellent black unit in Seattle also produced the play to great success. They had to modify the script because of their small stage and double up some of the parts, but the determination to do interesting, serious plays was typical of the Seattle unit.

Alvin Childress was the father of the mulatto women in the thing; [he] was really the linchpin of that whole damned thing. He was a brilliant actor. There were several good ones, but Alvin Childress, for my money, was the man who along with Rex Ingram made that play. . . . There were some damned good actors in Haiti. Some of them ended up doing horrible things. Alvin Childress ended up doing "Amos and Andy" in television. He was Amos. What can you say? A guy's got to eat. But he was a beautiful, sensitive actor reduced to playing Amos. It sort of made your stomach turn. A beautiful actor who did a beautiful role poised against a Rex Ingram who is . . . all muscle and noise.

LEONARD de PAUR, *musical director*

Jess Lee Brooks played Christophe, the black Napoleon, in the Los Angeles production of *Black Empire*.

No matter how good the actor who plays Henri Christophe, the interpreter of the role must work constantly. The audience must feel every moment the powerful impact of a tyrannical personality—tyrannical because he feels he must be so in order to place his race in its proper sphere of world activity. The projection of such power is a challenge to the best of actors, particularly when he has such moments of great human kindness and clear understanding.

ESTHER PORTER LANE, *Seattle director*

Director Claude Miller oversees the Los Angeles actors' rehearsal of the voodoo dance (opposite). Both of the West Coast casts of *Black Empire* studied voodoo chants and hand gestures along with histories of the island. The black history was one of the valuable side benefits of producing this play.

A play had been kicking around among the directors and no one wanted it. It was called Haiti, written by a reporter who was on the New York Times, who had written some melodramas for Belasco. This was a raw melodrama about Toussaint L'Ouverture and Christophe and the invasion by the forces of Napoleon to try to destroy the Haitian republic, the first Negro republic that ever existed.

Well, it wasn't a good play, but the idea that such a theme was to go untouched I just couldn't take. So I called the playwright up to my apartment. I said, "Look, this play should be done in Harlem, but if it is done in Harlem, I can tell you one thing. They will come right over the footlights and tear us to pieces."

"But," I said, "we can make a play out of this that they will love." And so we went to work, and we rewrote this play from top to bottom. It was about the victorious Haitian republic over the greatest army that had ever been in existence.

DuBois was a southerner, a real southern Cracker, and his play was about miscegenation, which excited him terribly. So finally, when the play was all finished and I was ready to go ahead with it, he said, "Listen now, Clark, listen. I've given in to you on every single thing but I want to tell you one thing right here and now that I demand, and that is that on that stage no white hands and no black hands shall touch." And I said, "Well, now, that's fair enough."

So, during the play the white and black actors didn't touch, but the encore was mine. When the curtain came up for the encore, the whites were among the blacks, holding hands, and that's how they took their bows.

MAURICE CLARK, *director*

Byron Webb, the technical director, confers with Perry Watkins, the set designer. Because of the racism of the unions, blacks were rarely found in the creative backstage jobs, but a few used the FTP to break through that barrier. Watkins also designed *Horse Play* and O'Neill's *S.S. Glencairn* while on the Project. After the FTP, he designed sets for revivals of *Big, White Fog* and *Run, Little Chillun*.

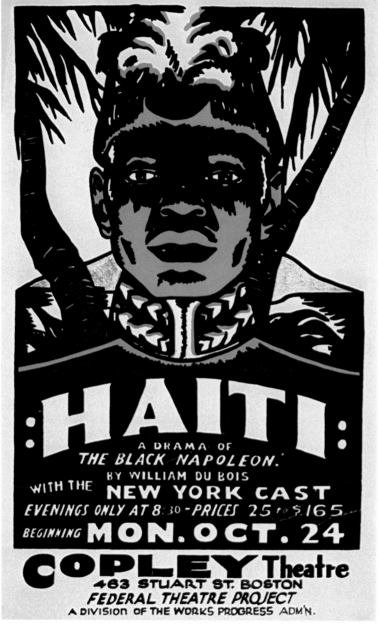

Haiti. Lafayette Theatre, New York City.

Of all the Lafayette productions that I enjoyed most—and I enjoyed many of them—I would have to say [it was] that thing of Du Bois', *Haiti,* the one with Rex Ingram, because of the people involved, and the sincerity of the project. I don't think it was great theatre. It was real melodrama, and Rex Ingram just flung himself around like a wild horse. But we had some excellent actors in it.

Maurice [Clark] was a wonderful man. . . . He used to come and eat in my house, and we used to sit and have great philosophical discussions about these people. He was fascinated by these Haitians whom I had known all my life. I had a father who made me learn black history as a child. When I was in high school I debated such things as: RE-SOLVED: That Toussaint L'Ouverture was a greater leader than George Wash-

ington. In the ninth grade, [I was] debating these things, literally; I mean in formal debate. So I knew these Haitians and he was amazed.

He said, "Do all young black fellows know these?"

I said, "Well, most of us do." Finally I had to break down and admit. I said, "You see, my father was from the Caribbean and he had a different attitude about education. I was sent to a school where black history was taught. I was taught black history in my home so that I have a different approach to these things than the average American who is not taught to know these people nor taught to regard them." And on that basis, we became wonderfully close for the time.

LEONARD de PAUR, *musical director*

Black Empire. *Seattle.*

Odette is told of her mixed blood by Christophe in this Connecticut production of *Haiti.* She must now choose between her French upbringing and black heritage; unlike the conventional "tragic mulatto" of the period, she is able to make a clear choice—to stay on the island—and survives.

Below: Canada Lee.

Rex Ingram was in Haiti. . . . He was a tremendous man, and he came in . . . and his foot hit the stage! He violated the silence, he violated everything. . . .

When Toussaint left to go . . . to Paris, he was turning his power, his leadership to Rex. And of course the sword was a piece of tin. Well, that's just the way Rex took the sword. . . . like it was a piece of tin, not like honed steel.

Canada Lee followed Rex down there [in the downtown version], and did a far better job, a far more understanding job.

I knew Canada [when] he was rehearsing, we got together and I pointed out to him the things that Rex had done so badly. He wanted to be an actor, and a good one. . . . It was much better from a theatre point of view, and from a very real point of view—it made some sense. I think towards the end it was like a madhouse, with the running and the dashing and the swinging— you know, it was comedy! . . . Well, let's say it was serious comedy.

ADD BATES, *actor*

Above: Toby Lietch is the man with the hat in his hand.

Black Empire *turned out to be a pretty good show . . . Toby Lietch was in that; he was an old-time vaudevillian. I used to see him when I was in my early twenties. He had a theatre downtown; Toby's Comedians they were called. I used to see him down there and I never dreamed I would be on the same stage with him, and there he was on the WPA. He taught us a heck of a lot of things about the stage that we would never have known if he hadn't been kind enough to teach us some of the tricks of the trade. It was very nice of him, and we were very good friends.*

JOE STATON, *actor*

HAITI AND BLACK EMPIRE   123

PINOCCHIO

T HE CHILDREN'S UNITS of the FTP pioneered in using adults, rather than children, to act in plays for young audiences.

In Yasha Frank's stage version of *Pinocchio,* first presented by the children's unit of the Federal Theatre Project at the Beaux Arts Theatre in Los Angeles in 1937, they had an immediate hit. The production played to capacity audiences for more than a year, alternating occasionally with other Federal Theatre children's productions.

Director Yasha Frank was extremely free in his treatment of the material, which was adapted from the original *Adventures of Pinocchio,* published in Italian in 1883 under the pseudonym of Carlo Collodi. Everything was sacrificed to simplicity and hilarity. Dialogue was used sparingly, but there was lots of movement, music, and general commotion to carry the action. The original Italian story of the wooden puppet who wanted to be a real boy had some elements that could seem tragic to children, but Pinocchio's unhappier adventures were glossed over quickly in this stage version. Mr. Frank himself wrote the dialogue in verse, and this was supplemented with an original musical score by Eddison von Ottenfeld and Armando Loredo.

Pinocchio was staged and written for children. Before the production was a week old, however, it became apparent that the attendance at some shows was 75 percent adult. Equally astonishing was the repeat business; it was quite normal for adults to see the show four or five times, and children seven or eight, a tribute to the liveliness of the production and appeal of the durable fairy tale.

Pinocchio's stage creator, New Yorker Yasha Frank, epitomized the wide

experience of some of the theatre people who found themselves working for the FTP. Frank had received a Ph.D. in psychology from New York University in 1923 and went on to join the production staff at Roxy's Capitol Theatre. Later he was recommended by Major Bowes to work under King Vidor and Erich von Stroheim on the MGM Board of Photography. In California, Frank also joined the Joseph von Sternberg production staff, then the Chaplin studio, and finally, wrote for Pathé Studios. This apprenticeship in the motion picture business was augmented by straight dramatic experience: he also directed sixty plays for the Potboiler Theatre in Los Angeles, known as the Provincetown Playhouse of the West Coast. Frank was serving as production assistant to B.P. Schulberg at Paramount Pictures when he resigned to become director of the children's unit of the Federal Theatre in Los Angeles, dubbing it "the chance of a lifetime." He also was in charge of the foreign department, producing plays in French, Yiddish, and Spanish for Los Angeles audiences.

In 1936 Hallie Flanagan appointed Frank as national consultant for Children's Theatre, a testimony to his creative and innovative approach to drama for young people. Frank's work with *Pinocchio* attracted so much attention that Walt Disney and his technical staff attended eight separate performances. Disney's next cartoon feature? *"Pinocchio,"* he announced.

In it there are sequences which approach more closely the classic works of Walt Disney than anything I have seen the stage produce. There is a beautiful undersea fantasy; there is a charming marionette sequence; there is, in fact, that kind of simple, imaginative fancy running through the production that not only delights a child's heart but touches responsive chords in the minds of the older and ostensibly wiser generation. . . .

Figures in colorful costumes move through the fanciful settings from the old carpenter's home through the public square into the puppet theatre, off to Booby Land, into the belly of the whale and back again. And not only the little wooden doll moves through these scenes, but cats and dogs and foxes and the blue-haired fairy queen . . . clowns and marionettes and soldiers and midgets. . . . . lions and goldfish . . . in short, almost every variety of flesh, fish, fowl or good red herring designed to warm the cockles of a child's heart.

ROBERT RICE, *in the* New York Telegraph, *January 4, 1939*

Pinocchio is tempted by a vista of Booby Land
in a set design proposed by Alexander Jones for
the New York production, which opened on
Christmas Eve, 1938, and continued until Congress killed the Federal Theatre on June 30,
1939. *Life* gave this production a color spread in
the March 27, 1939, issue. At the final New York
performance, Pinocchio ended the play inside a
pine coffin with the audience serving as
mourners. Children held placards with the
plaintive query, "Who killed Pinocchio?" as
stage hands demolished the set in full view of
the spectators.

Our first objective is to entertain children. We thought at first this would be difficult because they have been conditioned by movies and the radio to quite different things. Much to our surprise, our productions were greeted with enthusiasm by both adults and children. In some instances attendance has shown children outnumbered by adults three to one. This has vindicated my belief that everyone loves a fairy story, particularly one told with action rather than chatter.

Another objective has been to base each production on some character-building theme. In Pinocchio the lesson is that one should share his pennies with poorer folk.

Furthermore, we achieve success because we invite the children in the audience to take part in the performance. They are asked their opinion in critical situations and, afterward, they share in the distribution of goodies that have been used in the play. This creates for them an intensely personal experience and they remember the points that have been driven home.

The use of sensory devices sprang from an idea of mine when I was employed with Roxy in the Capitol Theatre in New York— to scent the air in the auditorium with orange blossom perfume when the trees were used on the stage in a revue. In Hansel and Gretel all five senses are utilized for the first time in any theatre, so far as I know.

We also utilize other devices to conform to behavior patterns, including the tempo and technique of vaudeville, such as Walt Disney does with his cartoons. We differ from Disney in not having a strong climax and overemphasis of the fear element. Our endings are always a series of anticlimaxes and our witches always turn out to be fairy princesses.

YASHA FRANK, director

When we first opened, when we first went into rehearsal for Pinocchio, I continued playing Gepetto by the skin of my teeth and finally opened it. Really I was very young, and I had a great many limitations as an actor. . . . [Yasha Frank] should have been playing Gepetto.

ALLAN FRANK

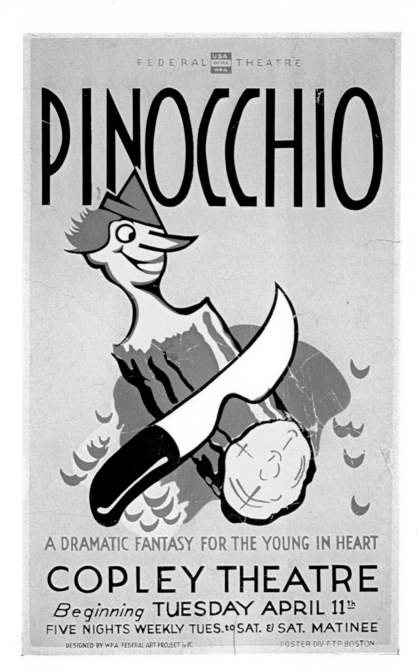

Yasha Frank had a great technique. He'd take all these old vaudevillians, who each had had a twenty- or thirty-minute act but were no longer up to the act, and he would take about three minutes of the climax of their act, which they were still able to do. He'd bring them into these children's shows, like Pinocchio. He'd run a dozen of just about three minutes of the essence of these great old vaudeville acts.

These old boys, their lives were wrapped up in that moment "when I wowed them in Altoona," and he'd take those moments and put them all together. He had such invention. There was a wealth of ability and creativity for what at first seemed very unpromising.

ROBERT SCHNITZER,
deputy national director

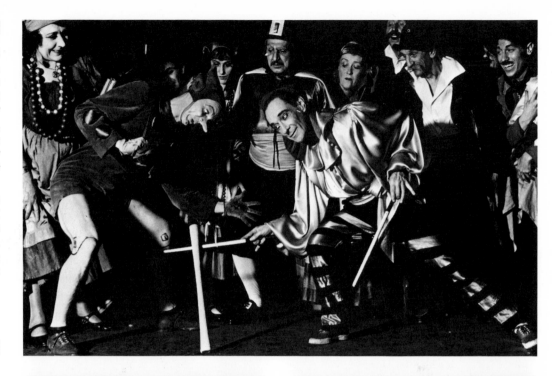

James Cochrane had fun with the "City Child" in this original sketch for the New York version at the Ritz.

Paul Cadorette designed both imaginative sets and costumes for the Boston show.

The lively, bright tones of this painting of Gepetto by Robert Sheridan accented the story-book quality of the costumes for the Los Angeles production.

VAUDEVILLE

STARTING SUNDAY APR. 12 8:30 P.M.

FEDERAL MAYAN THEATRE HILL AT 11th ST PHONE PR 0039

"FOLLOW the PARADE"

A MUSICAL REVUE AS MODERN AS TOMORROW

CAST of 100

ORCHESTRA OF 30

NITE 25 & 100 SAT. MAT 25 & 50

A FEDERAL THEATRES ATTRACTION

THE FEDERAL THEATRE PROJECT excelled in popular entertainment—circus, musical revues, marionettes, and nineteenth-century melodramas and romances—and from the beginning, vaudevillians were an important part of the FTP. In the first fifteen months of the Project, 24 percent of all activities involved vaudeville, and much of the free entertainment in hospitals, schools, and municipal parks was provided by the tumblers, dog trainers, aerialists, and singers and dancers who had been out of work. They were highly trained and experienced performers who had a tradition and a viable technique. Hallie Flanagan herself saw in the faces of the clowns—many of them former circuit headliners—the tragic-comic mask, which to her was "in a special way, the symbol of the Federal Theatre."

Early in 1936, Flanagan appointed Broadway actor-producer Eddie Dowling as director of vaudeville, with headquarters in New York City. It was to be his task to organize touring companies of musical comedy, vaudeville, and circus, and to route them throughout the country. His national program bogged down in governmental red tape, and Dowling soon resigned in disgust, but vaudeville flourished in many guises under FTP auspices.

In New York, the Variety Theatre, as the unit was called, put on highly successful vaudeville shows, musical comedies, and circus performances. Los Angeles, like Chicago, had an unusually large number of vaudevillians, and the units there became proficient at staging elaborate revues. Shows like *Follow the Parade, Revue of Reviews, Ready, Aim, Fire,* and *Two a Day* in Los Angeles and *Oh Say Can You Sing* in Chicago were made up of loosely connected medleys

Sketches by James Morcom, scenic designer (also on pp. 142-143). After Federal Theatre he designed the sets for Paul Green and Richard Wright's *Native Son*, produced by Houseman and Welles in 1941. Recently retired, Morcom was art director of the Radio City Music Hall for twenty-five years.

with a satirical intent. Frank Merlin's Variety Theatre described their presentations as vaudeville in form, but imbued with "socially minded" subject matter. They planned to treat such subjects as "Big Business," the "Negro Problem," and "How the Other Half Lives."

Los Angeles Director Edwin O'Connor later observed that the living newspaper was vaudeville with a basic idea. Certainly the snappy entrances and exits, the pauses, and the climaxes of the vaudeville technique readily found their way into other modes and formats. Half of the cast of the New York City living newspaper unit was recruited from vaudeville, and most of the children's units throughout the country were composed of former vaudevillians. The old rope or dog act became Saturday morning favorites, though the jokes had to be modified to fit the new audience. Other vaudevillians developed into skilled ac-

VAUDEVILLE   139

tors; in Seattle, lifelong vaudevillian Toby Lietch (whose legs had been broken in a barrel act) became the top character actor for that FTP unit.

Part of vaudeville's appeal was nostalgia. As Hallie Flanagan recalled, "The performance was not only gay and expert entertainment, but it had, due to the fact that so many headliners were playing parts which they had originated in other days, a between-the-lines emotional appeal."

In any case, experienced showmen, troupers, acrobats, musicians, magicians, comics, clowns, singers and dancers were out of work and "these for the most part were the people who became . . . the core of a new people's theatre."

The old vaudeville actors would just tear your heart out. You'd see some lady who looked like a wrinkled sixty-five, becoming coy and coquettish when she was next to you in the hall, working on you as an audience, singing "Just an Old Fashioned Garden." It was just great and it would tear your heart out.

Vaudeville in those good old days was based on one act and there were enough theatres that you might play it three or four years—you didn't have to think up another one. If you thought of one every four years you were in good shape.

PHILIP BARBER, *New York City supervisor*

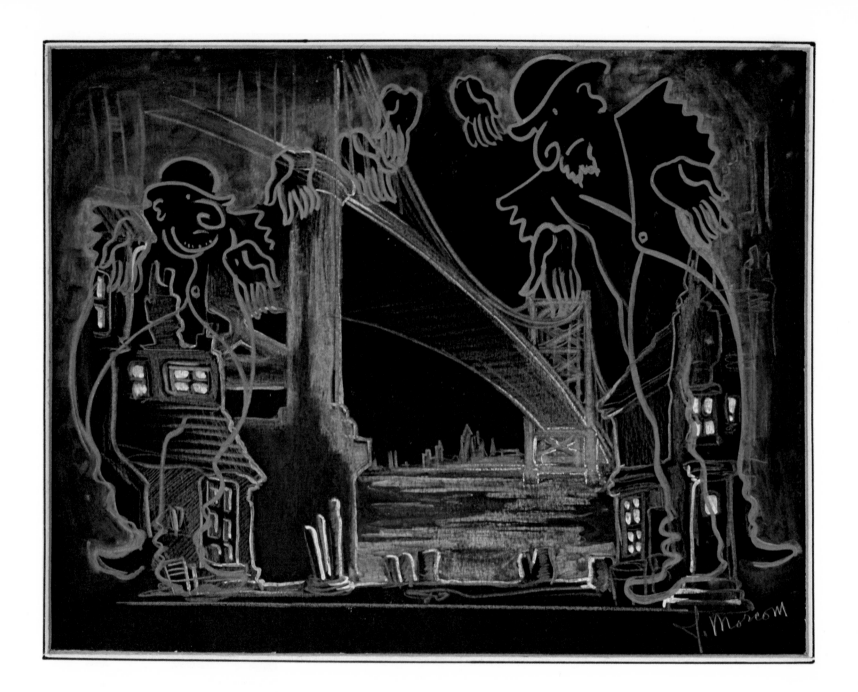

"GOLDEN SLIPPERS" · HELL SCENE · NELS ASTNER DESIGNER

What shall the premise [of the show] be? I answered: "Start from where you are right now. Start from where the people in the vaudeville unit are right now! Let's face it. They are unemployed actors! Play on that! Play on the fact that every single one of them longs to do a show again. That's all these dear people talk about when they congregate in our rehearsal hall. They talk about it anyway, so why not take them out of the rehearsal hall and let them speak out their longings and frustrations on the theatre stage? And instead of our off-stage rehearsal hall, the place on stage can be the living room of a typical middle class boarding house! This should be a prologue. Then—just as the different ones are sitting around complaining that vaudeville is dead, that they're—"out of the parade"—a young stage director will come into the living room. He'll have vital new ideas regarding the theatre. He definitely believes that vaudeville can be brought back, and he wants to present it in a new form. In—a musical show!

The show will be in two parts. First, the prologue, where in the living room of the boarding house, the actors will talk about wanting to do a show. The second half in a musical revue [where the actors] will be—doing the show. In this way the production will be a departure from the typical musical revue in that the comedy and satire will concern itself with one of the most important events of the day—unemployment—and, in fact, all topics that concern the world at the present time.

The entire production was tied together through a television idea and the master of ceremonies was presented as a television announcer. I felt this idea in itself would be an innovation, because—you know, it was 1935 and television had not as yet come into practical use.

The setup was an enlarged stereopticon projector. I knew a man who could do the mechanical work and he installed it in one of the boxes of the theatre on the right side of the stage. At performance time, the handsome television announcer—in tuxedo and black tie—inserted his head and shoulders in the rear of the large enclosed stereopticon, and in turn, his image was projected on the rear side of a huge transparent screen facing the audience. When his image first appeared on the screen, the audience applauded. And when he began to talk, the audience cheered, and Al Jolson (who was in the audience) stood up and said: "This is it! This is real show business!"

When I finished writing the premise of the show, I was so thrilled with the idea that the vaudevillians in this unit were going to get their wish: They were going to do a show! They'd no longer be—"out of the parade"—they'd be in it. They'd be—in the parade. Suddenly I thought, "that could be the name of the show. We're in the Parade! No—no—that would exclude the audience. They must be in it too, so—let there be a parade—and invite all—everyone—to follow the parade. That's it! That's the title—Follow the Parade!

EDA EDSON, *producer*

Individual vaudeville acts formed the backbone of some of the earliest Federal Theatre productions, as in these scenes from *Follow the Parade.*

Eda Edson knew what she wanted. She could scream but you had to learn that in the theatre. I enjoyed working with her. Of course, we went away with headaches from what she wanted.

CHARLES ELSON, *lighting designer*

Whether by using magic lantern slides to introduce acts *(Gaieties of 1936)*, a simulated television screen *(Follow the Parade*, far right*)*, or a series of "television announcements" from a side box *(Swing Parade)*, individual vaudeville acts needed to be tied together in a full-length production. The unity was effective in *Two-A-Day*, which traced the history of vaudeville, beginning in 1890. *Ready, Aim, Fire* (right), a satirical farce on the subject of war and dictators, was another approach. The Theatre Project itself was the narrative theme of Chicago's *O Say Can You Sing?* where both actors and officials of the Project were satirized, as well as its critics. Buddy Rich (bottom right) was featured in one of its many musical scenes.

It was a case, really, of doing a show because of your cast. The vaudevillians were on the Project, and our job was to do something with them. . . . All of us realized that you couldn't just do the old-time vaudeville, where one guy does his act, then another.

The show in which we really used the vaudeville talent was Two-a-Day. That is where, in my opinion—and I think most people felt the same—we began using vaudeville (because it was a show about vaudeville) in a social framework. We were able to do some actual parts of acts, but give them some kind of a setting, and also, in some cases, a completely new relationship.

There was an old vaudevillian called Bimbo, and his act consisted of constructing a tall bamboo tower, and he sat on the top of it in a barrel, quite a way up, and started rocking. And of course the audience said, "Oooh" and "He's almost falling," and finally he does. He tips it

over, and you think, "Oh, my God, he's gonna kill himself," and he jumps out of the barrel just in time and does a somersault. And that's his whole act. He's been going through his whole life doing this one thing.

We were doing a cavalcade of vaudeville, but we were also doing a cavalcade of America, starting back around the 1900s, the Gibson Girl and on up. So we used this for the stock market scene, the Depression. On one side we had people in a stock market, they were saying "The price is going up," and they were hollering and watching, as he is rocking. Well, we didn't do everything quite that clever, but that was the idea I'm trying to get at: where we could take something where you weren't just seeing that man doing his act, but you were getting a whole other value, a whole other level out of it.

GENE STONE, director

ANDROCLES AND THE LION

W HEN THE NEWS of Bernard Shaw's generous release of all of his plays to the Federal Theatre was announced, units all over the country clamored to do Shaw. In a letter to the playwright on May 7, 1937, Hallie Flanagan wrote of the FTP's plans to produce *Too True to Be Good* in San Francisco, *Heartbreak House* and *Caesar and Cleopatra* in Los Angeles, and she promised that the "Federal Theatre of the Air" had an ambitious program to be submitted for his approval.

Androcles and the Lion, always an overwhelming favorite with audiences, played in Denver, Los Angeles, and Seattle in the West and was produced by Harlem's Lafayette unit in the East. In vivid contrast to O'Neill's annoyance at the adaptation of his plays for Negro casts, Shaw encouraged Hallie Flanagan to seek Negro casts for his plays, "for Negroes act with a delicacy and sweetness that make white actors look like a gang of roughnecks."

The Lafayette production of *Androcles* proved Shaw right. The play, declared a hit by the *Amsterdam News*, ran for 104 performances. Directed by Sam Rosen, the original cast included Arthur ("Dooley") Wilson as the early Christian who befriends a lion with a burr in his paw, played by Add Bates. The kindness is repaid when Androcles and his friends are thrown into the arena with the lion, and a happy ending results. Hilda Offley as Magaera, Edna Thomas as Lavinia, Thomas Moseley as the Centurion, Daniel Haynes as Ferrovius, and P. Jay Sidney as the Captain, completed the list of main characters.

The production staff included Perry Watkins, the first black man to be allowed to join the Set Designer's Union; musical director Leonard de Paur, former assistant to Hall Johnson; Manuel Essman, who had worked on the set for the "voodoo" *Macbeth*; and lighting director Byron Webb.

The Lafayette version emphasized the character of Ferrovius, a powerful, inflammable man who ultimately chooses warlike Mars over the Christian God of forgiveness. Using what the *Amsterdam News* called "the innovation of racial music" for authenticity ("I'm Bound for the Promised Land" was substituted for "Onward Christian Soldiers"), the production was a rare combination of fun, sly wit, intelligence, and human concern.

Androcles *finally opened . . . and then Tamiris came up and put me to greater use in terms of movement. . . . It started making some sense; it had some movement. I was very active, you know* [as the lion]—*up and down—and they had to move when I moved. And Dooley* [Androcles] *was beautiful to work with!*

ADD BATES, *actor*

MEGAERA: Oh, you coward, you haven't danced with me for years, and now you go off dancing with a great brute beast . . . .

Lavinia (Edna Thomas) pleads with her small band of Christians to be strong in the arena (above) and assures Ferrovius (Daniel Haynes) that he will find his real faith in the hour of trial (above right).

ANDROCLES AND THE LION   155

156 ANDROCLES AND THE LION

ANDROCLES

FERROVIUS

Set and costume designs by Blanche Morgan, Seattle.

In Seattle, as in many other places, the Federal Theatre had not made sufficient effort to reach its vast potential audience—farmers, sailors, lumberjacks, small shopkeepers, housewives, the great mass of everyday people. The directors, Hallie Flanagan felt, had spent too much time trying to get the university audience. When George Hood, state director, showed Mrs. Flanagan the list of people to whom he sent invitations for first nights: "Just as fine a list as we used to have at the Metropolitan in the old days," he said.

"How many of them ever come?" she asked. When he said they were busy, that the theatre was far out, that they might come later, she remarked, "It's a shame to see a good show like *Androcles and the Lion,* playing to a small house when so many people would like to see it."

Then, of course, Perry Watkins was the archetypal example of what Federal Theatre meant to [the technical people] because he actually got into the Designer's Union. And that was like getting into the Holy See. He went down there, and Guthrie McClintic gave him a job doing Mamba's Daughters. And Bobby Jones, Robert Edmond Jones, vouchsafed him. He took the exam they have for those people. It's drafting, art, you have to practically design a show right there. And he passed it with flying colors.

LEONARD de PAUR, *musical director*

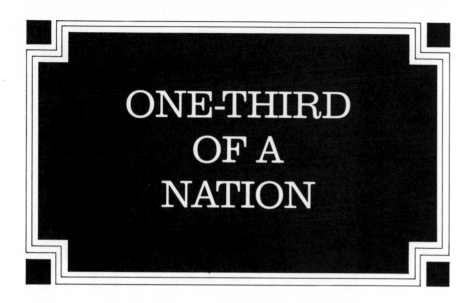

ONE-THIRD OF A NATION

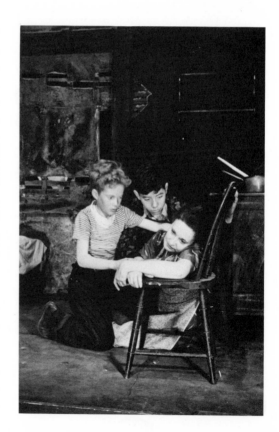

PROBABLY THE BEST known and most memorable production of the Federal Theatre was *One-Third of a Nation*. The New York production, which ran for almost all of 1938, was seen by over 200 thousand people, and was subsequently produced in ten other cities. Taking its title from Roosevelt's second inaugural address, the play dramatized the tremendous need for better housing in the big cities by focusing on slum conditions—disease, crime, needless suffering—their historical causes, and some possible solutions. The audience learned along with Mr. Buttonkooper, an Everyman figure, about the overwhelming demand for housing in Manhattan because of its rapid growth; the early land speculation by Trinity Church, which set a pattern for later speculators; and the inadequacy of civic ordinances. The educational process was directed by the off-stage, amplified "Voice of the Living Newspaper," who introduces scenes and provides information. The "loudspeaker" also cajoles, mocks, and questions various onstage characters as it challenges official responses to slum conditions.

The play fit well within Roosevelt's New Deal policies, although one radical character suggested that the only way slums would vanish was through a redistribution of income. The production did attract congressional criticism, however, for its references to specific congressmen and senators, and its support of the Wagner housing bill.

Arthur Arent, the author of all five living newspapers produced in New York, adopted more of the conventions of traditional social drama in this play than in his previous productions. The set was realistic, scenes were linked by

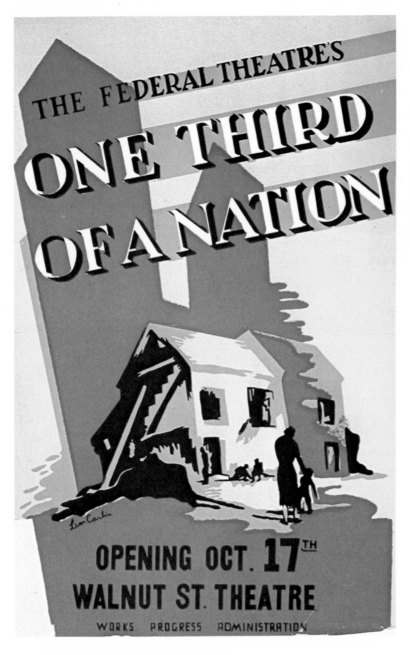

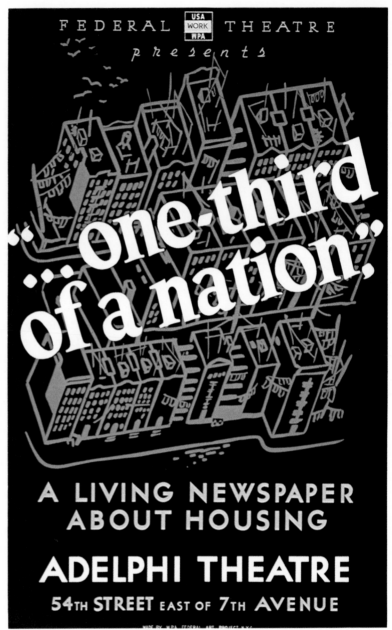

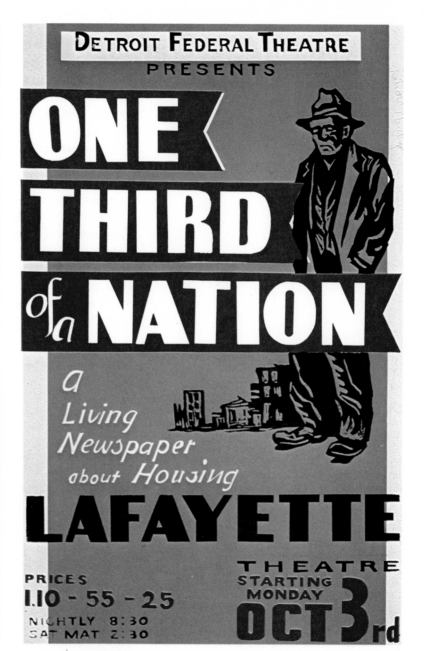

cause and effect, and the characters were more fully developed. Though a greater number of the scenes and characters were fictional than in previous living newspapers, the truth of the play was never in doubt. The script was completely documented, including references to real case histories, and, more immediately, the audience was confronted by a reconstructed, four-story tenement set. As every review and everyone's recollection testifies, it was this imposing set, more than any character or scene, that made slum life a reality.

Howard Bay, the designer, had reproduced the tenement in awesome detail, and with the use of steel scaffolding, it rose seventy feet high. The size alone was intimidating; the play then began with all the noise, smoke, and panic of a real tenement fire.

Bay's realistic set was actually his second design for the play. For a Vassar production the previous summer, he suspended above the stage giant symbols of tenement life. A leaky faucet, a roach, a toilet seat, and a broken fire escape were some of the objects that hung over and dwarfed the impoverished residents. In fact, many of the Federal Theatre personnel who saw the Vassar staging during their summer conference thought this abstract setting more effective than the later, more realistic, one.

That play had a smash and a power at Vassar that I never caught in New York. . . . Everything about the New York [production] was realistic, . . . but up at Vassar, under Hallie's supervision, it was all . . . the imaginative approach. For instance, the casting of the church wardens of Trinity Church, when they came to collect the ground rent, was very interesting.

In New York, they were played in full wigs, ruffs, whatever—and looked just the way actors often look when they're not at home in costume roles. At Vassar, the four church wardens wore a kind of tuxedo outfit, not the jacket, a flowing white shirt, a hat. A touch of the times, to remind you that even though they were a little anachronistic, these were church wardens from another day. They had the hat, they had the flowing white silk shirt, black trousers, black shoes, and one glove—just one ornamental glove from another day. And when they put out their hand for the church rent, you had a scene.

EMMET LAVERY,
director, National Service Bureau

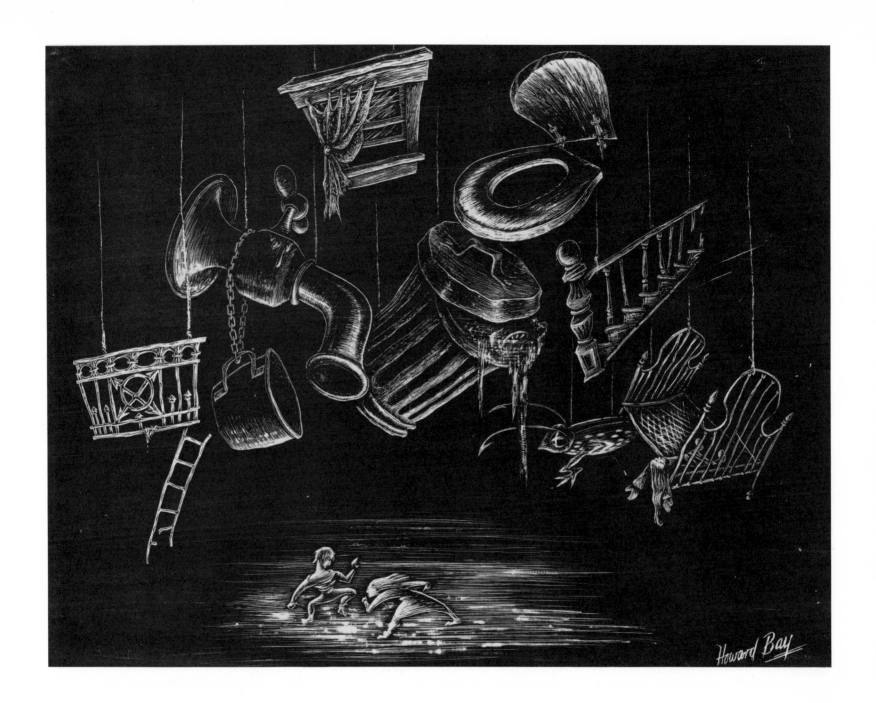

It was always very helpful if you attached swatches [of cloth] so that the costume department could put it right to work. You often went and got your swatches from them because they had all kinds of fabrics that had been donated by people in the garment district where we were. You could go through all the stuff they had and estimate what you could use in a given show and how much yardage there was. You would tell them, "Put that aside for this show which is coming up next month," then hope someone else didn't want it also. They were very cooperative. . . .

One-Third was fun to research. I spent long hours in the public library. Old files of magazines and newspapers gave a sense of reality and not so much [the] famous paintings of the period, which were over-dramatic. We were after a realistic look. If a fabric from the shop was too bright for the period, we would dye it. We could get plenty of dye and just brush it on so that the color would fit.

RHODA RAMMELKAMP BOLTON,
costume designer

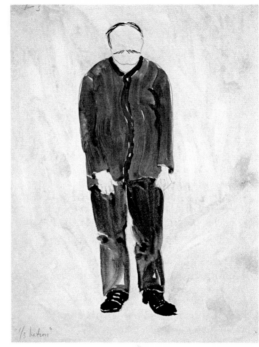

The FTP committed some of its best talent to the play to insure its success. Philip Barber stepped down as chief administrator of all New York City units in order to supervise this production. It was his suggestion that the set be realistic. He also chose as director Lem Ward, who was fresh from directing a successful FTP revival of Lawson's *Processional*. Ward did a brilliant job with *One-Third*, and with the boost from his work on the FTP, he quickly established himself as a top Broadway director before his sudden death from pneumonia in 1942.

They had a scene where they brought out a rug that was just green grass, a little spot of green grass out there. Then one person came out and bought this little section—there was a man there and he sold him a little section—and he stood on that. Then another man came along and brought another little section and stood there. Pretty soon there were people in each section. This guy would take out a razor and start shaving, this one would start doing something. There were about twelve people—first there was one person, pretty soon another, and a third, a fourth, a fifth one—and before you knew it you had a microcosm of the whole city. You saw in that little bit how thousands of people came to New York and what happened as a result. It was a fantastic production.

AL SAXE, *assistant director*

"We can not see that the housing problem is a government affair"

One-Third of a Nation *I particularly remember because we named senators in it, and it created more problems for me than any other living newspaper. Such and such a senator would come on—even if we didn't name him in person we made it very clear who he was—and say various things like, "Let them eat cake." [The quotes] were very damning to these senators, but they had said them in Congress, in the Senate, and we quoted them, happily. It had a tremendous impact—and it also had an impact on Congress . . . .*

We were in such a vulnerable position; we double-checked every quote. We would never say anything that hadn't been said. In One-Third of a Nation, *even though we may not give the names of the people calling out these lines, they were exact quotes from the Congressional Record. So there was no question about the truth of them. I thought it was a very forceful play.*

IRWIN RHODES,
general counsel for the FTP

Scenes from various productions across the country show the effects of slum life upon families: Seattle (upper left), Philadelphia (upper right), Portland (bottom left), and New Orleans (bottom right).

I suppose in a way [the New York set] was more theatrical. It wasn't basically a literal set, you know; the critics get all confused about these things. It was not a very literal set; it was a compilation of this, that, and the other thing—and a lot of real things out of tenements. Post was head of the Housing Authority—which is what they called it in those days—for the City of New York, and he was quite friendly with us, and with Eleanor Roosevelt and Hallie Flanagan. He allowed me to go around with him when tenements were subject to demolition. We had quite a bit of time, so I would say, "I want that balustrade, or that tin cornice," or whatever. And when they demolished it they set it aside, deloused it, sent it over, and we patched it onto the structure. The structure was the first use, I believe, of patented pipe scaffolding on the stage.

HOWARD BAY, designer

Local places and conditions were referred to in each of the cities where the play was produced. Two days before the play opened in the Walnut Street Theatre in Philadelphia, a tenement house in that city caved in. So, instead of a tenement fire at the opening of the production, a portion of the set collapses, crushing the helpless inhabitants.

(Music . . . Curtain up on bare house—one light very dim covers entire structure throughout scene. Music stops. . . .)

VOICE OF HOUSE: Well, I'm still here . . . There's been a lot of water under the bridge. We've had a few new Presidents and a Civil War—but I'm still here. You're curious, aren't you? You don't know where I am. Well, I'm here—inside the house. I AM THE HOUSE! (There is a pause. A spot picks up odd corners of the interior.) Do you see that broken balustrade? That crumbling plaster? And that sink down there under the steps? Do you see that rubbish piled up? That's me. I haven't changed a bit in all these years! Not a bit. In spite of their laws! LAWS! (Cackling laughter; sardonic.)

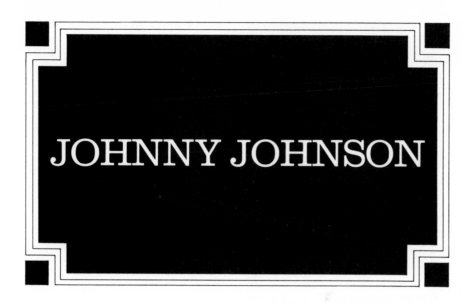

JOHNNY JOHNSON

Paul Green chose the name Johnny Johnson (played in the Los Angeles production by Brian Morgan) because more people by that name than any other had fought in World War I.

PAUL GREEN, with his belief in people's theatre, became one of the favorite FTP authors. At the time, Green was a philosophy professor at the University of North Carolina and a prolific playwright, especially of one-act folk and Negro dramas. *Johnny Johnson*, his antiwar play, was lavishly produced in Boston and Los Angeles, and a number of his folk dramas were performed nationwide. With one notable exception, the plays of his that Federal Theatre units chose had previously been done elsewhere.

Johnny Johnson was originally performed by the Group Theatre in 1936 under Lee Strasberg's direction, with the musical score composed by Kurt Weill. The critic Burns Mantle listed it as one of the ten best plays of 1936. The FTP production, in May 1937, attracted large audiences during the four-week run in Boston and six weeks in Los Angeles. The plot line is simple—Johnny Johnson sees no reason to go to war in 1917, but finally does go to "end all wars"; he almost succeeds in convincing the Allied High Command, before being declared insane. The Los Angeles FTP directors, Mary Virginia Farmer and Jerome Coray, described the play as "a series of fifteen scenes which vary in style and character from Gilbert & Sullivanesque vaudeville, slapstick, rural sketch, abstract stylization to straight realism—the whole interspersed with songs and musical numbers, some of which are tied into the action of the moment, some standing by themselves." The satirical, rather than angry, tone was appropriate to 1936 and 1937. A number of antiwar plays had been produced during the twenties and early thirties, but by the mid-thirties the world's steady progress toward another long, widespread war was becoming clear.

(And now the grey illumination of Johnny's face begins to die out. As it fades the other sleepers are heard moaning and twisting in the grip of an uneasy dream. And on their now tortured faces appears the same grey illumination, but Johnny's face remains in shadow. As if embodied forth by the restless sleepers' nightmare, the round muzzles of three great cannon push themselves slowly up over the parapet and then out and out until their long threatening necks stretch above the recumbent figures. They begin to sing in a queer outlandish trio harmony.)

GUNS: Soldiers, soldiers—
Sleep softly now beneath the sky,
Soldiers, soldiers—
Tomorrow under earth you lie.
We are the guns that you have meant
For blood and death—Our strength is spent
Obedient to your stern intent—
Soldiers, masters, men.
Masters, masters
Deep dark in earth as iron we slept,
Masters, masters,
Till at your word to light we leapt.
We might have served a better will
Ploughs for the field, wheels for the mill,
But you decreed that we must kill—
Masters, soldiers, men.

Soldiers, soldiers,
Sleep darkly now beneath the sky,
Soldiers, soldiers—
No sound shall wake you where you lie;
No foe disturb your quiet bed
Where we stand watching overhead—
We are your tools—and you the dead!—
Soldiers, masters, men!

The town's celebration of peace, in the opening scene, quickly turns into a call for war. Minnie Belle urges her beaux to be brave soldiers, then marries the one who stays home with a fake eye injury.

Posing as a messenger from the generals, Johnny tries—but fails—to stop the inevitable slaughter. Like the statue of Christ motioning for peace, Johnny is heard only by the dead and dying.

Johnny Johnson, written at the suggestion of the Group Theatre directors, is not a typical Paul Green play. More representative of his early work is *House of Connelly*, another play originally done by the Group Theatre and revived by the Federal Theatre in Los Angeles and Indianapolis. Writing about the fall of an old southern family and the rise of a new tenant-farm class, Green supplied two endings, one suggesting the formation of a new South as a result of a marriage between the old and new classes, the other detailing the predominately destructive values of both classes and the unbridgeable gulf between them. Green is also well-known for his one-act Negro plays. Seattle did *In Abraham's Bosom*; Hartford, *The Field God*; and New York, *Hymn to the Rising Sun*.

The Federal Theatre did sponsor the first performance of Green's *The Lost Colony*, which shaped the style and topics of his subsequent playwrighting. *Lost Colony* is an outdoor historical pageant about the founding of the Roanoke colony by Sir Walter Raleigh and the birth of Virginia Dare, the first Anglo-Saxon to be born in America. The play premiered in a WPA-built outdoor theatre in Manteo, North Carolina (the Outer Banks) in 1937 and has been shown there every summer since. Hallie Flanagan, a great admirer of Green, encouraged him to write a similar play about the early history of Virginia. The FTP closed before Green could finish the drama, but eventually Colonial Williamsburg chose *Our Common Glory* for their annual summer theatre. Green continues to write historical pageants for state and private outdoor theatres.

The design concept was to divide the stage virtually down the center, and to make it possible for the production to move as the director wanted it to move without any interruptions. The stage right side was the Connelly [side]. The stage left side was the tenant farmer section. The House of Connelly side was in rectilinear lines in old wood, and all that represented the house was just the symbol of the great fire stack with the portrait of General Connelly on it. The brown and the rectilinear, as it approached center, began to be less brown and less rectilinear and more curvilinear. When it got to center, it started to move into curves and into brown-greens and then greens. So that anybody that came out of the right was a Connelly and if he came out from the left he was a tenant farmer.

CHARLES ELSON,
Los Angeles set and lighting designer

Will Geer played the hypocritically pious Brother Simkin in the New York *Unto Such Glory*.

■ ════════════ ■

Mrs. Flanagan got the idea and she came down here, and stayed a few days. . . . We worked out plans with [Kurt] Weill and myself to write a play for the Federal Theatre, to be done simultaneously in seventy different centers. . . . Kurt Weill came down—he would stay here—and I'd write. . . . We got on near the middle of this thing, [with] great plans, and we were set. Then Mrs. Flanagan called up on the phone, and she said, "I've got terrible news," and I said, "What?" And she said, "They're going to kill the Federal Theatre."

PAUL GREEN, *playwright*

■ ════════════ ■

180   JOHNNY JOHNSON

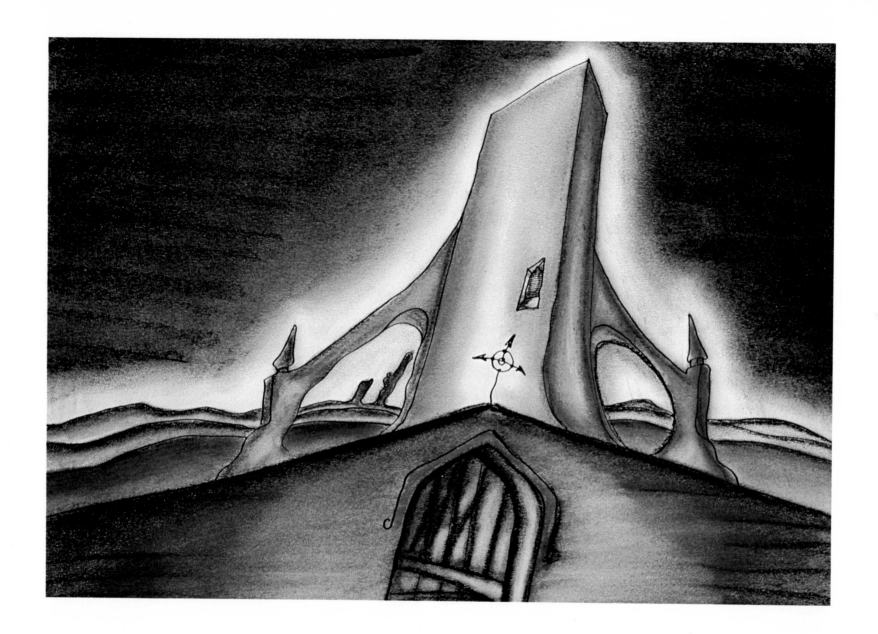

Frederick Stover, the chief designer of the Los
Angeles unit, created the backdrops used in the
fifteen scenes. Stover had been a student of
Donald Oenslager, who was the designer for the
original Group Theatre production.

The Field God, Hartford (left). Despite the destructiveness of his passions, which lead to murder and incest in this play, man can be a god—a Field God—in the angry, early plays of Green.

In Abraham's Bosom, Seattle (below). In the midst of the virtual slavery of the turpentine camps, the mulatto Abraham tries, despite repeated failures, to create a school for the Negroes.

Last of the Lowries, Jacksonville (above). Mauro, the last of the Lowries, has buried her husband and four sons, outlaw Croatians. First produced in 1920, *Last of the Lowries* is typical of Green's early folk tragedies.

My wife says why don't you get back to [the folk dramas], and I've heard people say "Why don't you do something worthwhile?" Well, I don't know. I keep doing [these historical pageants] that I'm workin' on now—I feel it is a challenge to try to get some real characterization, and I'm kind of stubborn. I have a feeling that these people, and this storehouse of material—somehow is important.

PAUL GREEN

Hymn to the Rising Sun, New York. Brooks Atkinson found the "passionate emotion" of this production "stunning."

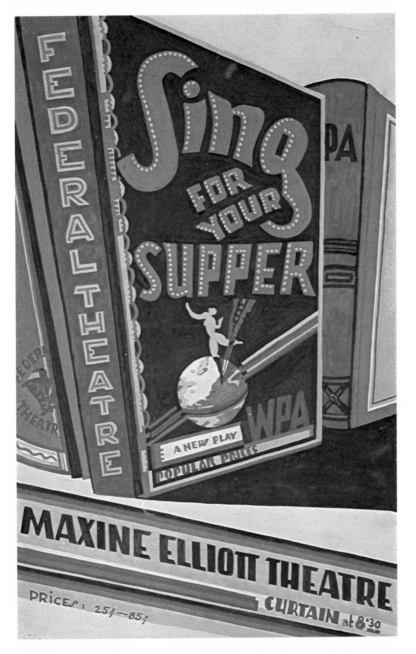

SING FOR YOUR SUPPER

AFTER EIGHTEEN MONTHS of rehearsals, *Sing for Your Supper* had become the object of some of the most violent attacks before the Dies Committee. The show seemed to epitomize what the committee (and later, Congress) deplored about the Federal Theatre: inefficiency, extravagance, and political satire. Directed by Harold Hecht, the revue began only with the conviction that the time had come for the Federal Theatre to try its hand at a musical. Unfortunately, the FTP had neither the stars nor the experienced writers on hand for such an ambitious undertaking, and the show moved along at a snail's pace.

Hallie Flanagan visited the set after a full year of rehearsals and saw only an hour and fifteen minutes of material. Without two or three core personalities to write music for, musical numbers were slow to materialize, and often when they did, both skits and actors were lost to private industry. Conflicts that arose from sheer incompetence frequently paralyzed the production.

Early in 1939, at the urging of Ned Lehac and others, George Kondolf signed Charles Friedman to pull the show together and get it ready for the stage. When the play opened in March 1939, at the Adelphi, Brooks Atkinson's review was titled "Federal Theatre's *Sing for Your Supper* Officially Concludes Rehearsal Period."

The objectives, to me, seemed to be political rather than creative. We always had that conflict before we could get the show on. One day I came to see a run-through of a part or all of the show, I don't remember, and I noticed a brilliant young dancer in the show. I suggested to the director and the people in charge that we do something about this man, surround him with better material because he was so good. They agreed to do that. Several weeks later I came and he was no longer in the cast. I asked, "Why?" "Well, he didn't work well; he was uncooperative, or something." It was Gene Kelly! I'm sure he was uncooperative with that group and was just plainly fired.

GEORGE KONDOLF,
supervisor of the New York City FTP

"PAPA'S GOT A JOB"

(Lyrics by Robert Sour and Harold Rome; music by Ned Lehac)

Papa's got a job!
Ain't it lucky—ain't it swell?
I ran all the way home to tell—
I'm so happy it's just like ringing a bell.
Papa's got a job!

Papa's got a job.
Do you know just what this means?
There'll be soup in the soup tureens,
And today we can say good-bye to those beans.

Night after night "Papa" had been lifted up by his friends and neighbors celebrating his new job, but on the night the Project closed the producer froze the action and announced to the audience that Papa was losing his job "at twelve o'clock tonight." When the performance ended, the audience and cast joined in singing "Auld Lang Syne."

Mayor Frank Hague's antired, antiunion campaign in Jersey City keeps young lovers apart. "Her Pop's a Cop" but her lover is in the CIO.

I was asked to go into Sing for Your Supper, *and that thing was like bloodletting. A few shows were never permitted to open on Federal Theatre, so you had to go to work, and you would rehearse, and rehearse, and rehearse, and rehearse! There were two suicides on Federal Theatre, just because of boring repetition! And rejection—because of not opening.* Sing for Your Supper *was an endless struggle to open.*

You kept rehearsing and rehearsing, and rehearsing. . . . [There] was a form of "incestuous boondoggling" going on: Getting your money. Meanwhile, the upper echelons were holding back. The show was ready to open, going to costume, going to sets, and nothing happening.

During that particular time, I got a call from Clurman . . . for Golden Boy. It was an opportunity for a young performer to step right into a proven show. It was a hit. I played it on Broadway for about eight weeks, then the show went to London for two months, and we had to leave, for we already had set a tour which took us to Chicago and other cities . . . When we went back to New York, Sing for Your Supper *hadn't opened yet. Now that's tragic, tragic for the people. I don't know how the studio didn't explode among them during all that time. That's really burning up every capacity, artistically. I don't know how they survived; I couldn't have.*

WILL LEE, *actor*

Mary Merrill had designed costumes for two of the FTP's more notable successes, *Prologue to Glory* and *Big Blow*. For the Provincetown Playhouse unit of the Project, she also costumed the casts of *Tobias and the Angel* and *Cherokee Night*. *Sing for Your Supper*, with its particularly huge production numbers like "Papa's Got a Job," presented a real costuming challenge, which she met with a subtle and charming array of city-inspired designs. The animal costumes were for a number called "Spring."

"The Ballad of Uncle Sam" survived *Sing for Your Supper* as "Ballad for Americans," and was performed under many circumstances. Paul Robeson sang it on the radio to a nationwide audience. And in an ironic twist, the 1940 Republican National Convention used it as a theme song.

Paula Laurence with young actor Bowen Tufts, later known as Sonny.

When I got the formal notification that I was to do Sing for Your Supper, they told me to report at nine o'clock for rehearsal at so-and-so hall—in fact, the rehearsals took place all over town in halls and lofts and churches and auditoriums, the bottom of schools, and everywhere else. . . . The first thing I had to do was go see Hal Hecht, who was the producer of the show . . . and I went to see Bob Sour, who wrote a lot of the lyrics for him. Then I met John LaTouche. He wrote the "Ballad for Americans," and was having to change the lyrics a lot. The show was in rehearsal so long, that to keep it timely, he had to put new things in it. But the Earl Robinson music, of course, was stable.

The first time I went [to rehearsal] there was a tremendous hall on the Jewish East Side somewhere, and there was Anna Sokolow, one of our young choreographers. There she was, just giving them practically a basic lesson in body movement. And this is what the Federal Theatre actually did. There was education, they prepared you to get you in the swing of whatever they were doing . . .

TONY BUTTITA, *press agent for the FTP*

"LEANING ON A SHOVEL"

(Lyrics by John LaTouche; music by Lee Wainer.)

We're not plain every day boys,
Oh no, not we.
We are the leisurely playboys
Of industry,
Those famous little WPA boys
Of Franklin D.
The Republicans insist we're gay deceivers.
Their anger is so terrific,
While the other workers slave away like beavers
They say we're merely—soporific.
So tonight you can detect us
As we're seen in the GOP prospectus—:

Here we stand asleep all day
While F.D. shooes the flies away
We just wake up to get our pay
What for? For leaning on a shovel!

In the forest the CCC
Is also snoozing peacefully,
Cause only Hoover can make a tree
While we keep leaning on a shovel!

When you look at things today
Like Boulder Dam and TVA
And all those playgrounds where kids can play
We did it—by leaning on a shovel!

We didn't lift a finger
To build the parks
That you see in every city.
At home we always linger
And read Karl Marx
If you don't believe us—ask the Dies Committee.

Miles of roads and highways, too,
And schools and buildings bright and new—
Although it may seem odd to you
We did it—by leaning on a shovel!

You politicians voting against our crew,
Can't you see folks getting wiser?
You ought to be a'toting a shovel, too,
The way you shovel up the same old fertilizer.
Let the papers have their say,
Let the elephant snore and the donkey bray,
If we can get things done this way—
Hurray for leaning on a shovel!

Murial Watts (in the polka-dot blouse) toured the whole world in a vaudeville act, "The Woman With a Thousand Faces." She was featured in a series of Williams and Walker productions, the most successful being *Bandanna Land*. An original Cake-Walker, she taught the younger performers some of their steps in "Opening Night."

The Monster-Dictator in "The Last Waltz,"
choreographed by Anna Sokolow with music
composed and arranged by Alex North.

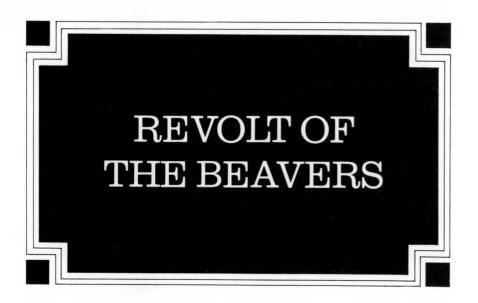

REVOLT OF THE BEAVERS

At first the Professor (Joseph Dixon) hopes to placate and teach the Chief through a fable, but eventually he joins Oakleaf in the revolt.

R EVOLT OF THE BEAVERS, a children's play by Oscar Saul and Lou Lantz, can still generate arguments about whether it is a typical fairy tale or Marxism veiled as Mother Goose. Hallie Flanagan, after reading the script, wrote that it was "very class conscious," but she and the rest of the FTP were still surprised by the critics' charges when the play opened on May 20, 1937. Brooks Atkinson wrote in the *New York Times* that, "Many children now unschooled in the technique of revolution now have an opportunity, at government expense, to improve their tender minds. Mother Goose is no longer a rhymed escapist. She has been studying Marx; Jack and Jill lead the class revolution." This play seemingly confirmed the suspicions of FTP critics that the children's unit was a center of radical activity. Many of its members had previously acted in various workers' theatre groups. The play subsequently became prime evidence for the House Un-American Activities Committee in its search for Communist control of the FTP.

In the play two small children dream that they visit Beaverland, where "The Chief" and his cohorts force the other beavers to supply the bark for a wheel that produces clothes and food. The chief and his pals are the only ones with blue sweaters, roller skates, and ice cream. When the working beavers object, they are replaced by "barkless" beavers. Oakleaf, an exiled beaver (played by Jules Dassin), a beaver professor, and the two children organize a beaver club, throw out the chief, and establish a new order where all things are shared by all.

Whatever its politics, the play was undeniably an imaginative and enjoyable production. With its bright set and costumes, lively music, and actors on roller skates, the play attracted full houses of both adults and children. Despite its drawing power and theatrical merits, *Revolt of the Beavers* closed after a month's run. It was simply too controversial for the embattled FTP administrators.

It was not a really revolutionary thing. . . . I don't think it was that dangerous. It was really marvelous. The kids loved it. We had marvelous reactions from the kids, because they would cheer the good guys and they would boo the bad guys. Ben (the Boss) for example, had a marvelous throne as the King of the Beavers. It was a barber chair with a lot of levers. You know how when you sit in a barber chair you can move the levers and go up and down and swing around? He had one of those, and they loved seeing it. He may have been a bad guy, but he had the chair. The chair was connected with a slide, so that when he wanted to go down and talk to anybody, he'd just press a lever and the front of his chair went down and he slid right down. It was so imaginative, so different from any children's theatre at that time. Still to this day it would be considered an extraordinary work that Oscar Saul and Lou Lantz had done. It was inventive, and beautifully directed and beautifully acted by very good actors.

JOHN RANDOLPH, *actor.*

PINE CONE: But the chief of all the beavers
He gets all the bark we make.
All he does is pull the levers
While we work until we ache.

BIRCH: So we're poor unhappy beavers
Working busy as the bees
While he sits and pulls the levers
And gets fatter if you please.

While Ruff, Tuff, and Gruff (Allan Frank, John Randolph, and Elena Karam) guard the children and Oakleaf, the Chief's police and the Scaly brothers confront the protesting workers.

Oakleaf (Jules Dassin) plots the chief's overthrow with his new friends Paul (Sam Bonnell) and Mary (Kathleen Hoyt).

Sam Leve designed Beaverland and the costumes.

The response to the Beavers was an almost hysterical one. No child in his right mind, and most children are in their right minds, could possibly have been influenced by this play in any way, because essentially it was in all of its important aspects a real classic kind of Robin Hood—good guy versus bad guy—story, in the most primitive and obvious sense. But because of a particular philosophical orientation, there were kinds of specific spikes, almost guidelines, that were set in that gave it a particular flavor and made it recognizable to some people. I remember that Brooks Atkinson became furious about it: This had been written by people who had been reading Marx. But it was not really in any important aspects Marxist. It was a primitive and basic story of good and bad—good guy, bad guy, the suffering poor, the oppressive rich—which is classic. It's all through history. There was some very authentic poor boy background, in terms of some of the images, story patterns, and thrusts, but the essence of it was very old and very familiar. There really wasn't anything new about it.

LOU LANTZ, *playwright*

LIFE AND DEATH
OF AN
AMERICAN

L IFE AND DEATH OF AN AMERICAN was one of the three major FTP shows running in New York when the Project closed. *(Pinocchio* and *Sing for Your Supper* were the other two.) The success of this production proved how the Federal Theatre could be more than a relief agency: It could stage shows that the commercial theatre thought too risky, and it could offer valuable opportunities for talented young people.

George Sklar had originally written the play in 1937 for the Theatre Union, which had produced some of his earlier works *(Peace on Earth,* with Albert Maltz, and *Stevedore,* with Paul Peters). When the Theatre Union dissolved, the Federal Theatre offered to produce *Life and Death of an American.* The play opened on May 19, 1939, at the Maxine Elliott Theatre under the direction of Charles K. Freeman. The musical score and songs were written by Earl Robinson and Alex North, who later became successful song writers and composers for both theatre and film. (Robinson composed the music for the famous "Ballad for Americans," and North was nominated for a number of Academy Awards.)

Jerry Dorgan, the main character in the play, is the first American born in this century, twelve seconds after midnight, January 1, 1900. His family is poor, and his college hopes are cut short when his father dies and he must drop out of school to support his mother. During World War I he learns to fly, and in the boom twenties he earns an aviation drafting job through his hard work and intelligence. But the Depression follows, and Jerry loses his job. In the original version he goes back to stunt flying, but in the version revised for the FTP, he is shot to death during a labor demonstration.

Arthur Kennedy and Eleanor Scherr in *Life and Death of an American.*

The experimental design of the play and the lively staging by the FTP made many of the reviewers think of it as a living newspaper. A chorus of chanters introduce the scenes, comment upon Jerry's hard times, and take part in the frequent crowd scenes. According to Hallie Flanagan, *"Life and Death of an American* had been declared by Piscator to be the most superb stage production he had seen in America."* Despite differences in style and theme, the play was often compared to Kaufman and Hart's *American Way,* primarily because both plays capture turn-of-the-century life in their early scenes.

It was a very touching, warm, statement, an Our Town *before* Our Town *was written. It was a semistylized production going from realism into narration, and into stylization and stylized scenes. It was my first gentle singing experience on stage, and I'm not a singer at all. One of the songs from that production stayed with me. We stood behind a rocking chair, left and right of the woman who was playing the mother, and we helped her sing:*

Sleep my Baby, sleep my child,
Sleep and have no fear;
Mother's watching over you
Daddy's always near,
Joy will be your lot,
We will make it so;
All the things we never knew
Will be yours to know

PERRY BRUSKIN, *actor*

George Kondolf welcomed the play. He was so excited about it, and I was quite delighted to have it done on the Project, because it would reach a bigger audience for one thing, and two, because it was a very demanding play technically. It had an enormous cast, it was a multimedia thing long before multimedia things were being done. I mean, not only songs, but dance and movement; it was a multiscene production and had fluidity that was almost cinematic. Broadway couldn't afford to do a play like that; it was an art thing. The one misgiving I had about the thing was that Kondolf and, I guess, the director, Charles K. Freeman, wanted me to rewrite the ending.

GEORGE SKLAR, *playwright*

George Sklar.

What were the significant influences on scene designers? Max Gorelik was quite influential; it was Max that introduced Brecht. Piscator was here in the New School. The big exhibit that Lee Simonson put together at the Modern Museum in 1935 was influential because the Russian models were fantastic at that time. They sent over a dozen or so models that were really amazing. . . . We were allowed to experiment, too. If we wanted to try something, we tried it. . . . In the mid-thirties, late thirties, we did the open stage for the first time in a large set. Not that you couldn't find an isolated show ahead of it, but the open stage—the frank use of space in building out the apron, the formalism that the stage is only so big and so deep and you see it and you see the lights—all of those things we did in a large way and fairly consistently. I don't know what came first. The dramaturgy started breaking up episodes into strings of vignettes, fragments, where you had to use the open stage.

HOWARD BAY, *set designer*

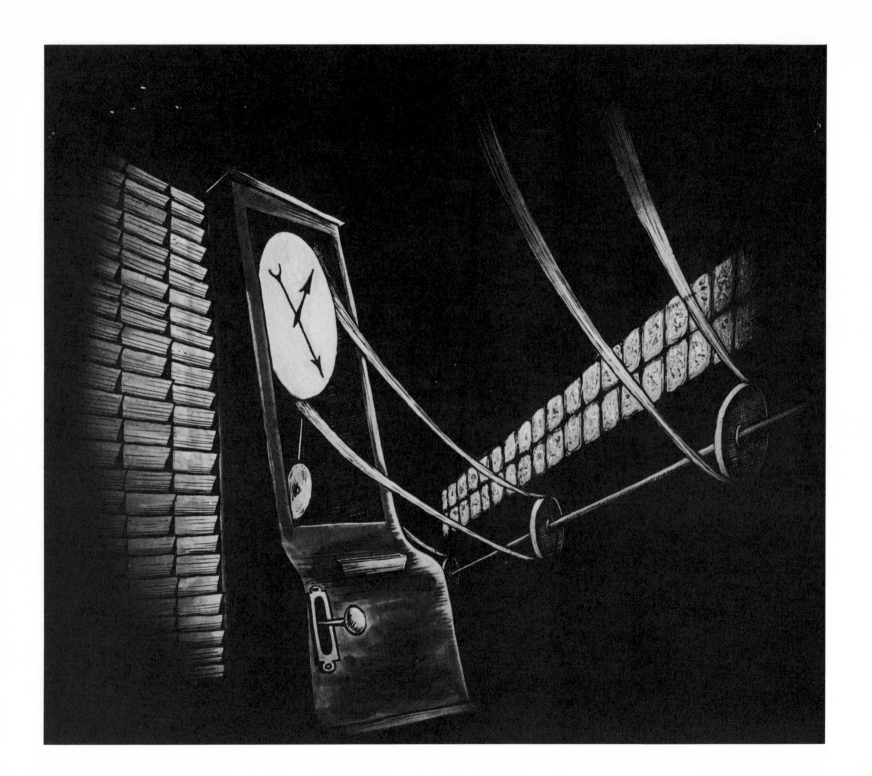

JERRY: Poor Pop—I hope he gets well quick—
(*he crosses himself*) I shoulda got those shoes
for him—A year—Jesus—guess I'll hafta leave
school now—get a job. I can't let her go to
work—she ain't strong—she says she will—
doesn't want it to make any difference—yeah,
well, it'll make a difference all right—plenty.
Jeez, I don't wanta go in the shop—just when
things are beginnin' to break my way—gettin'
good marks—football—Jeez, it ain't fair—go in
the goddam shop and yuh won't see the gang—
Mary—Christ, why should I? Well, whadda yuh
gonna do about it? Whadda yuh want, the ol'
lady to go work for yuh? They ain't done enough
for yuh, have they? Pop says to take care of
her—Yeah, and it won't hurt yuh, either. What
the hell!—It's only a year. Pop'll get better and
you'll go back—and you'll be a sophomore instead of a junior, so what? What's all the steam
about? Anybody'd think it was the end of the
world or something—What's one year in my
young life! Nuts! First down and ten to go! . . .
One thing—I won't feel so funny about takin' the
ol' man's dough for college. . . . Jeez, I bet it'll
feel funny goin' back with the freshies . . . (*A
factory whistle blows—the orchestra starts
playing. A line of workers, shoulders bent,
lunchbox in hand, trudges rhythmically
across stage.*)

(*Jerry gets up from the stairs and falls in with
them. Suddenly we hear the whirr of machines.
The time-clock clangs. The line stops. The men
turn front. To the accompaniment of the
machine rhythms, which are accented by the
music of the orchestra, they execute stylized
work movements—repeating them monoto-
nously. As they do so, they keep up a steady
chant of "one-two-three-four—one-two-three-
four." Single voices come out of it.*)

FIRST VOICE: In she goes and watch your
finger—Bang! In she goes and watch your
finger—Bang!

ALL: One-two-three-four—one-two-three-four.

SECOND VOICE: Monday, Tuesday, Wednesday, Thursday, Friday, Saturday, Monday,
Tuesday.

FIRST: On your toes, there, I mean you!
Who do you think I'm talkin' to?

THIRD: Fourteen hours every day—
Gotta work to get your pay!—

SECOND: Monday, Tuesday, Wednesday,
Thursday, Friday, Saturday, Monday, Tuesday.

FIRST: In she goes and watch your finger.
Bang! In she goes and watch your finger. Bang!

FOURTH: Dirt and dust, and dust and dirt—
Watch out there, or you'll get hurt!

FIFTH: (*Singing*) My bones are achin',
my back is breakin'.
I feel so weary and blue.

FOURTH: January—

THIRD: February—

SECOND: March—

FIRST: April—

SECOND: Thursday—

THIRD: Friday—

FOURTH: Saturday—

GIRL: Come on, clock, do your stuff,
Come on, baby, I've had enough.

JERRY: Come on whistle, come on, blow
Come on whistle, we wanna go!

ALL: Bones are achin', backs are breakin'—
Tired and feelin' low—
It's gettin' late and we're sick of workin'—
Blow, whistle, blow!

To get a bit of bread to eat,
We come here every day,
We sweat and strain and bend our backs
To get our weekly pay.

Shop walls hold us like a jail,
From early morn till late;
That whistle shuts the bars on us,
At night it opens the gate.

Saturday's pay day, Sunday's rest,
The Saturday sun is low;
Come on, whistle! Toot that whistle,
Blow, whistle, blow.
Come on, whistle! Toot that whistle!
Ten more seconds to go;
Seven, eight, nine and ten,
Blow, whistle, blow!
(*The whistle blows. The music comes to a stop.
The workers stop their movements.*)

FIRST WORKER: Here she comes—

GIRL: Ooh, money, money, money, money,
money.
(*They all make a rush for Amy, who comes on
with a box of pay envelopes.*)

SECOND WORKER: Hyah, babe!

THIRD WORKER: Are we *glad* to see yuh!

Though he had been with the Group Theatre before, Arthur Kennedy was still an unknown when Charles Freeman picked him for the lead in *Life and Death of an American*. After he auditioned nearly 200 actors, Freeman chose Kennedy because he had the "feeling and appearance" of Jerry Dorgan. He was hailed by the New York critics for his part, and Sidney Howard quickly offered him a part in his next play, *Summer Night*. Kennedy went on to play numerous Broadway roles, including the Tony-award-winning role of Biff in *Death of a Salesman*.

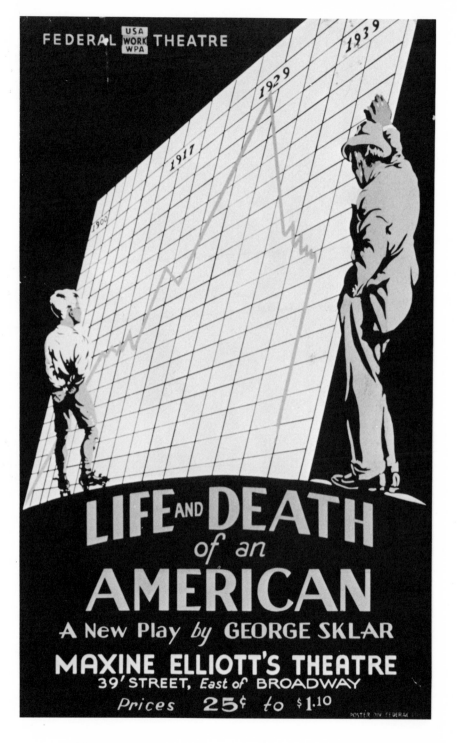

LIFE AND DEATH   211

DANCE

Modern dance in America had always played against an active challenging background, beginning with Isadora Duncan's protest against the artificial formalization of ballet and its lack of human emotion. The Duncan style of dancing was democratic and antiauthoritarian and characterized by the expression of vital human themes. The pioneering efforts of Isadora, Ruth St. Denis, and Ted Shawn to free dance from exclusive groups were responsible for the growth of interest in modern dance that the country experienced in the thirties and in which Federal Theatre itself was to play a pioneering role.

When the Federal Theatre Project was formed in August of 1935, it was Helen Tamiris, one of the most vocal and active modern dancers, who took the lead in getting dancers themselves recognized as a group, rather than as components of the Theatre Project. The idea of bringing modern dance to masses of people who had never before been in a concert hall or theatre inspired Tamiris, who devoted herself to keeping the Project going for the next three years. She so identified her own career with the Project that she sacrificed her independent career to it. But she was able to convince Hallie Flanagan that modern dance, as a creative form, could express vital ideas. Music, costume, and lights—all aided in the projection of an idea; everything was focused on the content of the dance.

Actually, Hallie Flanagan needed little persuading and almost single-handedly moved Congress to support an independent dance unit. In January 1936, the Dance Project was established with Don Oscar Becque, a producer in existing dramatic units, as director. Executive committee members included Doris Humphrey, Felicia Sorel, Gluck Sandor, and Charles Weidman—an im-

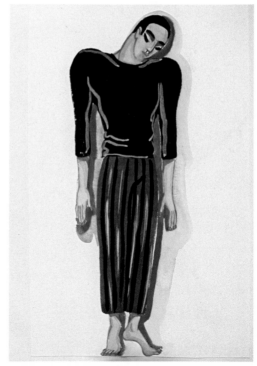

Costume designs (opposite) for *How Long Brethren* and (below) for *Let My People Go.*

pressive group. The staff of musical directors was equally distinguished. Donald Pond, the young English composer formerly musical director of the Dartington Hall School of Dance-Mime was appointed chief musical director, and Wallingford Riegger and Genevieve Pitot were named as associates.

Given 150 thousand dollars by Congress to mount eight productions in six months, the New York Dance Project hoped to present its first show by the end of February. To those familiar with the work involved in dance production, designing, rehearsing, and producing eight productions in six months seemed an impossible task. Indeed, it wasn't until the end of June that three matinee performances were finally staged at the Majestic Theatre in Brooklyn: Charles Weidman's *Candide* and Doris Humphrey's three dances, *Prelude*, *Parade*, and *Celebration*. Tamiris' own production of *Salut au Monde*, an extension of her *Walt Whitman Suite*, wasn't produced until August. Becque's highly original *Young Tramps* soon followed. Impossibly high aims, red tape, changes in personnel, and inadequate budgets, not to speak of artistic jealousies and rivalries, all contributed to the delays and postponements. By November there was a stormy public hearing in which Becque was violently attacked for a multitude of sins,

not the least of which was his espousal of "a common denominator technique" that would take in dance movement of all types. Dancers who had struggled for years to perfect their own techniques were incensed and vehemently condemned such artistic interference. Also contributing to the sagging morale were the rehearsals of *Young Tramps* and *The Eternal Prodigal*, that had gone on so long that even the dancers were rebelling. In December Becque finally resigned. Lincoln Kirstein, his successor, stayed only a short time, and after that the dance unit was assimilated with the other small New York City units directed by Stephen Karnot.

In spite of the artistic success of such shows as *How Long Brethren?* the Federal Dance Project was attacked as being dominated by the "mad modernistic dancers," as well as engaging in political agitation. The first sit-in strike in the American theatre was led by Charles Weidman when all projects were ordered to fire one-third of their personnel to conform to congressional cutbacks. By October of 1937, the cuts were made, and the Federal Dance Project was again merged with the Theatre Project.

A dance sequence about poverty, racism, and death, *How Long Brethren?* by Tamiris (shown opposite), was based on seven black protest songs. The production included a large chorus and full orchestra. The ten-week run was unprecedented for a modern dance program, and the audiences frequently interrupted the action with their cheers. The program was revived the following year.

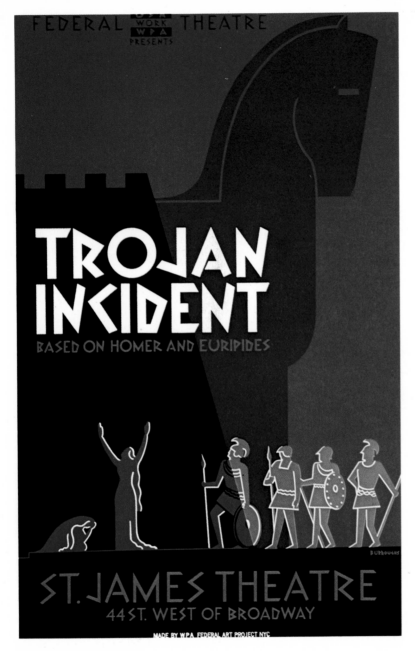

The dance units still functioned even after they had been absorbed back into the FTP. One large dramatic work that emerged before the whole project shut down was Tamiris' dance about the Spanish Civil War, *Adelante*.

What a really thrilling dancer [Tamiris] is when she breaks free from the moorings of sobriety and lets what a European critic once called "the magnificent lust of motion" take possession of her! Long ago she stated her conviction of her dance as a dance of affirmation, and who is to contradict her? But it is none of your pious and self-conscious affirmations, dealing in noble principles and deathly truths; it is rather, the declaration of an entire delight in the dynamic actualities of the present, however wanting they may be in cosmic significance. That this is merely frivolous or wanton cannot be maintained in face of the dance itself, for it captures and brings to the surface that relish in living which most of us allow to be submerged all too easily in the welter of trying to get along. . . . There is a vitality, a warmth, about her that relates her movements inevitably to human living, when she allows it to remain free from superimposed literary and philosophical dominance. . . . What we need from her is more and more of that affirmation upon which she has laid so much stress; and we need it not only because it is part and parcel of her art but also, since she is interested in "social content" in her dancing, because there is probably nothing anywhere to be found in the way of content that is more strongly social.

JOHN MARTIN, *New York Times*

I may be prejudiced in favor of the pantomimic dance, because I have found that my gift as a dancer is essentially tied up with my dramatic talent as an actor, or—let us better say—as a mime. The modern mime must be a modern dancer, and as such his entire body must be alive. This cannot be acquired by emotional experience, only by hard physical training. It may be best called bodily awareness. In order to test this bodily awareness in one of my dance compositions, I went so far as to exclude the face, i.e., the facial expression, completely from the pantomimic presentation.

JOSE LIMON, *dancer*

Charles Weidman and Doris Humphrey choreographed two programs each for the Federal Theatre. Weidman's *Candide* was performed in tandem with Tamiris' *How Long Brethren?* in 1937. One of the young dancers in the company was José Limon (opposite, above, and below, with Lily Verne). His later career became closely associated with Doris Humphrey (opposite, in a solo). In the following year, Weidman choreographed and starred in *Race For Life* (right), one of the series of dance pantomimes based on Thurber's *Fables*. Doris Humphrey's first FTP performance was a repeat of her popular *Prelude, Parade, Celebration*. In 1938 she created for the FTP one of her finest dances, *With My Red Fires*, performed on the same bill as *Race For Life*.

The Chicago Federal Theatre Project had a number of important choreographers: Ruth Page and Bentley Stone, Grace and Kurt Graff, and Katherine Dunham. They attempted to popularize modern dance by creating full-length productions based on folklore and current social problems. Their productions on topical themes were occasionally superficial or conventional, but their other work was marked by its good humor and infectious energy. They also provided movement and dances for such Chicago hits as *Swing Mikado* and *Oh Say Can You Sing*.

Frankie and Johnny was the highlight of the first edition of the Federal Ballet. Choreographed by Ruth Page and Bentley Stone, the dance was a conscious appeal to new audiences. Also on the bill was a Page-Stone production of *American Pattern*, which described the struggle of a woman dissatisfied with her conventional life.

Guns and Castanets, a dance version of Bizet's *Carmen*, was the main feature in the second edition of the Federal Ballet. The Page-Stone production set the action in the midst of the Spanish Civil War.

Katherine Dunham's *L'Ag Ya*, the climax of *Ballet Fedre*, was an energetic portrayal of love and festival based on the folk-life of Martinique. John Pratt, her husband, designed the costumes.

In Los Angeles Myra Kinch supervised and choreographed a group of about twenty-five dancers, which included Bella Lewitzky. Her programs, divided into three parts, usually included some opening satires, a piece on an American theme, and something more dramatic, like *Let My People Go*, a depiction of racial violence and suffering. Modern dance was rare in Los Angeles, but Kinch's productions were well received. Besides dance concerts she also choreographed many of the Los Angeles plays, including *Johnny Johnson* and Yasha Frank's *Aladdin*.

Left: The Los Angeles Company in *Anthem*. Below: Myra Kinch and Clay Dalton in *An American Exodus*, also shown opposite.

The dancers in the Concert Group are working toward group expression, a blending of individual personalities and techniques into a modern medium of expression. In the past, American dancers (much as designers have bowed to the decrees of Parisian dressmakers) have followed the precedents set by European choreographers. Even music was necessarily of foreign composition if it were to be given serious consideration. American choreographers are now striving toward a point of view that is essentially American, with music composed from the movements of the dance, or arrangements applicable to the period in question. An American approach offers the choreographer a wealth of episodes for either serious or satirical consideration. . . . American Exodus was a dance impression of the pioneer seeking a new land, its cultivation, the building of new homes, the harvest, the burden and nostalgia of the women, love, and finally the joyous festival celebrating a full existence.

MYRA KINCH, *choreographer-dancer*

In our first concert we were using Scarlatti, and I had choreographed a whole group of satires. . . . The whole dance had to be ready for dress rehearsal in a couple of days, and they called and said, "We can't get clearance, we can't pay the royalty, we can't use the music." And I said, "But the dance is made, we've let it go on, it's too late to change it."

"We can't use it."

My husband [Manuel Galea, pianist-accompanist for the unit] took the score, and he composed a piece of music that the dancers could dance to. It was almost identical—not identical, naturally, it couldn't be, or you couldn't use it. It didn't even sound exactly like the other, but it was so near that everything fit in, and to this day I still use that music—it works very nicely for a lot of things.

I remember he spent hours, all night long, and then sent it out to be copied at the last minute, and then practically the day before we opened, the dancers had to do this piece of music they'd never heard. But it worked!

The second program, Let My People Go, was a ballet that my husband composed the music for. We did it in San Francisco, with the San Francisco Symphony, and we had a hundred-piece symphony orchestra. It was a fantastic experience. It was about the Negro people and about a lynching, but it was done very "modern dance"—suggestive of the idea. I guess this was one of the things that [made them decide] I was doing propaganda. Well, I certainly don't believe in lynching, never did and never would. . . .

MYRA KINCH, *choreographer-dancer*

CHRONOLOGY

The Federal Theatre Project officially opened on August 27, 1935.

Black Empire opened at the Mayan Theatre, Los Angeles, on March 26, 1936.

Injunction Granted opened at the Biltmore Theatre, New York City, on July 24, 1936.

Horse Eats Hat opened at the Maxine Elliott Theatre, New York City, on September 26, 1936.

It Can't Happen Here opened simultaneously in twenty-two theatres across the country, on October 27, 1936:

Doctor Faustus opened at the Maxine Elliott Theatre, New York City, on January 8, 1937.

Revolt of the Beavers opened at the Adelphi Theatre, New York City, on May 20, 1937.

Johnny Johnson opened at the Mayan Theatre, Los Angeles, on May 28, 1937.

Pinocchio opened at the Beaux Arts Theatre, Los Angeles, on June 3, 1937.

Processional opened at the Maxine Elliott Theatre, New York City, on October 13, 1937.

S.S. Glencairn (including *Moon of the Caribbees*, *In the Zone*, *Bound East for Cardiff*, and *The Long Voyage Home*), opened at the Lafayette Theatre, New York City, on October 29, 1937.

Androcles and the Lion opened at the Federal Theatre, Seattle, on November 1, 1937.

One-Third of a Nation opened at the Adelphi Theatre, New York City, on January 17, 1938.

Haiti opened at the Lafayette Theatre, New York City, on March 2, 1938.

Run, Little Chillun opened at the Mayan Theatre, Los Angeles, on July 22, 1938.

Big Blow opened at the Maxine Elliott Theatre, New York City, on October 1, 1938.

Sing For Your Supper opened at the Adelphi Theatre, New York City, on April 24, 1939.

Life & Death of an American opened at the Maxine Elliott Theatre, New York City, on May 19, 1939.

The Federal Theatre Project closed on June 30, 1939.

INDEX

Composed in Clarendon by New Republic
Books, Washington, D. C.

Printed and bound by Dai Nippon Printing
Co., Ltd., Tokyo, Japan.

Photography by David Kasamatsu.

Book design by Susan Marsh.